ON THE MOVE

AN ADVANCED ENGLISH COURSE

by Peter Buckley
and Luke Prodromou

Oxford University Press 1988

Oxford University Press
Walton Street, Oxford OX2 6DP

Oxford New York Toronto Delhi Bombay
Calcutta Madras Karachi Petaling Jaya
Singapore Hong Kong Tokyo Nairobi Dar es Salaam
Cape Town Melbourne Auckland

and associated companies in
Berlin Ibadan

Oxford is a trade mark of Oxford University Press

ISBN 0 19 432811 2
© Oxford University Press 1988

Second impression 1988

First published 1988

Typeset by Tradespools Limited, Frome, Somerset.
Printed in Great Britain by Richard Clay Ltd, Bungay, Suffolk.

Introduction

If you are studying *On the Move* your level of English will be above that of the Cambridge First Certificate but not as high as the level of Cambridge Proficiency. This book is designed to bridge the gap between these two levels by improving your general skills of speaking, listening, reading and writing in English. At the end of the course you will be ready to study for the Proficiency exam, if you wish.

How the book is structured

● The book is divided into nine sections, each on a particular theme. Within each section, the four units examine the theme from different, and sometimes unexpected, angles.
● Units usually begin with a 'warm-up' discussion to get you thinking about a topic then lead on to a reading text or listening passage, followed by exercises which help develop your language skills. Each unit focuses on a particular point of grammar and finishes with a writing task.
● The list of contents at the front of the book tells you what language skills you will be practising in each unit, the activities you will be doing (e.g. role-play) and what area of language you'll be studying in detail (e.g. reporting verbs).
● On page 203 you will find the tapescripts of the listening passages but it is essential that you do not look at these until you have completed the relevant unit

How to get the most from the course

It is important to use the right approach when learning a language, to make your learning as efficient as possible. Section One looks at different aspects of learning English and will provide you with a lot of practical advice about how to learn. In addition, you should think about the following points:

Your dictionary
At this level you should be using a monolingual dictionary, for example, the *Oxford Advanced Learner's Dictionary of Current English*. Make sure you read the introduction to such a dictionary because it will explain just how much useful information you can get from it: pronunciation, verb patterns, special uses, word-building with prefixes and suffixes. There is even a book which will help you get the most out of your dictionary: *Use Your Dictionary* by Adrian Underhill (Oxford University Press).

Your notebook
Since *On the Move* is arranged by theme, try listing your vocabulary by theme group; it is far easier to recall and use words grouped in this way. It is a good idea to record the grammatical category of a new word, for example, noun (N), verb (V), adjective (adj.), and the most common words it is placed with, for example, a *tall person* but a *high building*. You can also build other words by adding or taking away prefixes and suffixes (see page 92 of this book), for example, *attractive* (adj.), *attractiveness* (N), **un**attractive (opposite). By using these techniques, you can actually acquire several new words for every single word you learn.

Grammar
You may also want to record points about grammar in your notebook or file. You should note sample sentences together with typical errors, and give a reference to the unit of *On the Move* and to a grammar book, to assist in revision. In this course many of the grammatical labels, for example, '*it* as preparatory subject', are those used in the grammar book *Practical English Usage* by M Swan (Oxford University Press). You can also build up a list of your own errors, by carefully examining the homework corrected by your teacher and referring to a grammar book or the unit of this book. You may like to record your typical mistakes at the back of this book so that you can easily check them before you hand in the next piece of work. Many students at this level make the same mistakes over and over again so if you can eliminate these, you will have achieved a lot.

A final word on learning

Learning is very much an active process. It is unfortunate that a lot of classroom activity takes place sitting down because this can induce relaxation. You should actually be mentally running and jumping throughout the lesson. Take bits of language, think about them, try to use them, compare them to what you've previously learnt, ask questions about them.

We hope what we've put in this book will make your learning what it should be – an enjoyable process. Have fun!

Contents

1 Are you a good one?

3 Me and the animals

4 Foul play

5 It takes two

bright sparks

7 On the dark side

8 Do it yourself

9 On the move

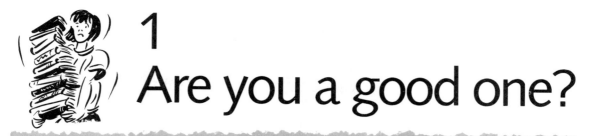

1
Are you a good one?

1 Speaking

In pairs, each look at one picture and cover the other picture. Describe your picture to your partner and find the differences.

2 Listening

Locating specific information

a   You will hear an interviewer asking two teachers about their students. Listen to the two interviews and mark with a tick (√) the points which the teachers mention in the table overleaf. (You will see from the example that the teacher may refer the same point to the good student and the bad student.)

Points	Good student		Bad student	
	Teacher 1	Teacher 2	Teacher 1	Teacher 2
Speaking	*tries to speak English in class*		*likes to speak own language*	
Homework				
Mistakes				
Experimenting with the language				
Reading				

Note-taking

b Listen again and complete the table with notes of what the teachers say about each point (one has been done for you as an example).

c Which of the following statements do you think the two teachers would agree with? Say why.
1 The good language learner is a willing and accurate guesser.
2 The good language learner is usually not inhibited.
3 The good language learner has a strong drive to communicate, or to learn from communication.
4 The good language learner is constantly looking for patterns in the language.
5 The good language learner practises.

Vocabulary

d Listen to the interviews again and work out the meaning of the following expressions. They are given in the order you will hear them.
1 'it's always a good sign'   4 'stick his neck out'
2 'it's a great help'   5 'off his own bat'
3 'and peep over at his neighbour's paper'

e Which of the following adjectives did the second teacher use to refer to the good student? Listen and note the phrase in which the adjective appears.
1 afraid   3 willing   5 reluctant
2 eager   4 keen   6 interested

f   Make sentences for each of the adjectives in exercise 2e.
Example:
The good student is not afraid to make mistakes.

3 Speaking

a   In groups, make up your own questionnaire to find out if someone is a good student or not. Make twelve questions.
Example:
Are you willing to read a lot?   Yes ☐   No ☐

b   Now form pairs with members of another group and exchange questions. Return to your group and compare your results. Which group has better students?
Compare the results of all the groups. Which group has the best students?

4 Grammar   Identifying relative clauses

a   The relative pronouns *who*, *which*, *that* in the examples below are the **subject** of the relative clause. Draw lines to show which pronouns are used with non-human nouns and which with human nouns.

The book   **which**
                that   *provides all the answers is in my room.*
The student   **who**

b   The relative pronouns used as the **object** of the relative clause are *whom* (in formal English), *which* (in formal and informal English), and *who* and *that* (in informal English). However, the relative pronoun is often omitted in informal English, for example:
The book **(which)**/**(that)** *I've chosen is on the table.* (Informal)
The student **(who)**/**(that)** *I sat next to failed the exam.* (Informal)
But:
Those students **whom** *we might classify as 'good learners' have a strong drive to communicate.* (Formal)
Look at the sentences below and delete the relative pronoun wherever possible.
1 I know the student that wrote this.
2 The short skirt which the girl wore upset the headmaster.
3 The parents that wrote to the headmaster are outside.
4 The class complained about the teacher who gave too much homework.
5 I met the girl that the teacher ran away with.
6 The teacher about whom there were complaints has retired.
7 The students who passed bought the teacher a present.
8 The parents that the teacher hit are in hospital.

c When the relative clause introduced by the relative pronouns *who*, *which*, *that* is in the **passive**, we can omit more than just the relative pronoun, for example:

The book (which is) selected by the committee will be announced tomorrow.
The student (who has been) caught cheating is in hospital.

Look at the sentences below and find those where the relative clause is in the passive. Then make the deletions as in the examples above.

1 I feel sorry for the teacher who was sacked last week.
2 The student who wanted to see you is downstairs.
3 The boy that was expelled for smoking is waiting outside your flat.
4 The book which everybody wants to read has gone missing.
5 The classroom which had been used for the exam was covered in paper.
6 The teacher removed the skirt which had been causing all the trouble.
7 The student who was appointed head pupil had an excellent academic record.
8 The headmaster congratulated the teacher who had been promoted to assist him.

d In **4a** we looked at relative pronouns which were the subject of the relative clause. We cannot shorten such clauses in the same way that we did in **4b** and **4c**. We cannot say:

× The student wanted to see you is downstairs. ×

But we can shorten the clause by using the pattern **noun + adjective + infinitive + main clause**, for example:

The student eager to see you is downstairs.

Using the following adjectives, change the sentences below in the same way.

eager	keen	unwilling
willing	afraid	reluctant

1 The student that wants to practise will learn quickly.
2 The student that doesn't want to speak in class won't make much progress.
3 Any class that wants to do a lot of homework should do well in exams.
4 The student that doesn't mind doing extra work at home will make a good learner.
5 Those who don't want to listen to the teacher won't learn much.
6 Students who don't mind learning from their mistakes have the right idea.
7 Any student that doesn't want to experiment with new language won't get very far.
8 No student that wants to learn should miss this book.

e Complete the sentences below, using one of the patterns in **4a – d**. For each sentence it may be possible to use more than one pattern.

1 The student .... has been in the same class for three years.

2 Teachers are never happy working with machines ....

3 Universities are full of students ....

4 .... will learn very quickly.

5 Any book .... is certain to be popular.

6 .... is coming to see you.

7 .... you taught ....

8 Any student ....

5 Writing

Imagine you are thinking of applying to a language school in Britain to join a summer course. Make notes of your answers to the following questions, then write a letter to the school, introducing yourself and asking them to send you details of their courses.

- Personal data (name, age, occupation).
- How long have you been studying English?
- Where did you learn your English?
- Have you ever been to Britain before?
- Why do you want to take a course in English?
- What do you expect from the course (language practice, social activities)?
- How much do you expect the course to cost you?
- Do you want to learn about Britain and the British way of life?
- What facilities, apart from classroom teaching, do you want the school to offer you?
- Have you attended other language courses? If yes, give your impressions.

Think about how to divide the paragraphs of your letter. Possible headings for paragraphs could be:

1 Information about yourself
2 Your reasons for applying
3 Request for information

UNIT 2 LEARNING TO LISTEN

1 Speaking
In pairs, look at the illustrations and discuss:
Which of the activities illustrated do you find more difficult to manage in English? Why?

2 Reading

Gist reading

a Ignoring the blanks, read the following text once quickly to see if the writer agrees with the opinions you expressed in the first part of this unit.

One of the most important features that distinguishes reading from listening is the nature of the audience. . . . . (1) the writer often does not know who will read what he writes and will almost certainly not be present when it is read, he must attempt to be as clear as possible. Time can be taken to plan the piece of writing, over a number of hours, days or even weeks, so that it is eventually organized into some sort of logical sequence of events or ideas. The logical sequence will be emphasized by the use of connecting words which help the reader to follow the writer's line of thought. When we speak, ... (2), we normally have very little time to plan what we intend to say. . . . . (3), we may begin speaking before we have even decided what to say. Our thoughts then tumble out in anything but a logical sequence. Since we are actually addressing our audience face to face we may omit some of the information we believe our audience shares. . . . . (4) the more familiar we are with our audience, the more information we are likely to leave out. In any case they can always stop and ask a question or ask for clarification if we have left out too much.

A reader, ... (5), cannot do this but can at least attempt comprehension at his own speed; that is to say, he can stop and go backwards or forwards, refer to a dictionary or just stop and rest. When we listen we may have to work hard to sort out the speaker's thoughts by referring backwards and forwards *while* the speaker continues. As the speaker struggles to organize his thoughts, he will use filler phrases to give him time to plan. . . . . (6) these fillers, he will still make mistakes, even grammatical mistakes, and repeat what he has already said or temporarily abandon one topic for another before returning to the original topic. His speech (particularly if it is informal speech) will be characterized by a limited range of grammatical patterns and vocabulary and the use of idioms to convey some general meaning quickly. It should be clear, ... (7), that the listener has to take an active part in the process by ignoring the speaker's repetitions and mistakes, and by seeking out the main information through recall and prediction. To keep the process going smoothly he also has to inform the speaker that he has understood without actually interrupting. This is normally done by facial gestures, such as nodding, or by short noises which indicate comprehension. You can verify this by falling silent when listening on the phone. The speaker will eventually stop and check that you are still actually on the other end of the line.

Text-attack skills

b Read the text again and choose the appropriate link word to fill the blanks.

1 However / Since
2 similarly / however
3 Alternatively / Indeed
4 But / And
5 nevertheless / however
6 In spite of / Because of
7 soon / then

Note-taking

c Write notes under the following headings to show the differences between spoken and written language as mentioned in the text.

Spoken language	Written language
Unplanned	Planned

Locating specific information

d Find at least four points in the text which explain why listening may be difficult in a foreign language.

Inference

e The writer says:

1 '... the more familiar we are with our audience, the more information
   we are likely to leave out.'
   Discuss what sort of information he is referring to.
2 '... to inform the speaker that he has understood ... is normally done
   by facial gestures ... or short noises.'
   Discuss what gestures and noises you use in your own language to do
   this.

3 Listening

Gist listening

 **a** You will hear an example of informal speech. Listen and decide which
one of the following is true.
The speaker was asked to tell a story about one of his most

1 exciting
2 dangerous } moments.
3 boring
4 amusing

Locating specific information

b Look at the table below. It shows some characteristics of spoken
language. Listen again and in groups, complete the table with other
examples from the text.

Characteristic	Text examples
filler	*'well, um'* ....
repetition	*'a great, great job'* ....
simple link word	*'but'* ....
idiom	*'cost them a fortune'* ....
false start	*'He said, er, I said ...'* ....
simple vocabulary	*'a big event'* ....

Vocabulary

🔲 **c** Listen again and try to work out the meaning of the following
expressions. They are given in the order you will hear them.
1 'a really big deal'
2 'cost them a fortune'
3 'we are sitting there, preening ourselves'
4 'she was going on rather a lot'
5 'we knew it couldn't be a flop'
6 '. . . I was absolutely staggered by this . . .'
   (Can you think of other adjectives to replace 'staggered'?)

Appreciating style

d Informal speech contains simple lexical items, especially adjectives.
Can you replace the following examples from the story with other more
formal adjectives to fit the story?
1 a *big* event   4 a *great* job
2 a *great* conference   5 a *great* moment
3 a *wonderful* job

4 Grammar Reporting verbs

a The use of direct speech is a characteristic of informal story-telling. In the
story you listened to, the woman said to the man:
'You did a wonderful job.'
The man could report this by saying:
She said that I'd done a wonderful job.
She congratulated me on doing a wonderful job.

Match the expressions in the speech bubbles with the correct reporting verb.

to advise   to promise   to deny   to warn
to remind   to refuse   to apologize   to suggest

1 I'll be there
really I will.

2 I don't know
anything about it.

3 I'd see a doctor
if I were you.

4 Don't forget
your appointment.

5 If you do that
again, I'll hit you.

6 I will not give in
to your demands.

7 I'm sorry, I've
made a mistake.

8 Why don't we
phone to check?

b Reporting verbs follow several different patterns (compare *She said that . . .* and *She congratulated me on . . . -ing*). Look at the table below and add more verbs from the following list to each part of the table. Some verbs can be used in more than one way.

accuse (of)	convince	offer	remind
admit	deny	persuade	suggest
advise	encourage	promise	tell
ask	insist (on)	blame	thank (for)
confirm	notify	warn	

Reporting verbs that *do not* need an object when a verb phrase follows.	Reporting verbs that *do* need an object when a verb phrase follows.
verb + *(that)*	
say (that)	inform (someone)(that)
verb + infinitive	
refuse to	order (someone) to
verb + *-ing*	
apologize for ...ing	congratulate (someone) on ...ing

When you have finished, check your table with other students.

c Report the expressions in **4a** using the correct verb and pattern.
Example: *She promised to be there.*

d In pairs, write an expression to match each of the following reporting verbs. Write the expression only, then exchange it with another pair. Report the expression you are given, using the correct verb and pattern.

admit	confirm	deny
convince	inform	notify
encourage	persuade	

Example:
Pair A 'No, I'm afraid we never study English outside the classroom.'
Pair B 'They admitted (that) they never studied English outside the classroom.'

5 Writing

Pre-writing

a Study the following table and put the link words listed below in the appropriate columns.

Giving examples	Sequence	Reason	Result
for example	*firstly*	*for this purpose*	*so*

Addition	Contrast	Comparison	Reference back
besides	*instead*	*similarly*	*this*

also   thus   nevertheless   likewise
however   since   meanwhile   therefore
on the one hand/   they   in the same way   such as
on the other hand   finally   in contrast   it
moreover   furthermore   in addition to   these
such

b Using the completed table, fill in the blanks in the following text.

Listening is in many ways more difficult than reading. One reason for .... (1) is that the reader can stop, look up a word, and think about what she or he is reading; the reader can .... (2) slow down, if the information is dense. The listener, ... (3), has no .... (4) advantages: .... (5) the fear of new words is more acute in listening than it is in reading. Students often panic when they hear the first unknown word in a listening passage; .... (6) feeling becomes paralysis by the third or fourth unknown item. Even the best students underestimate the difficulties in listening; .... (7) often lack the learning strategies which are essential to effective listening.

.... (8) listening makes great demands on the grammatical as well as the vocabulary skills of the listener. .... (9) the foreign learner is unable to predict the pattern of a sentence through its grammatical signals he has a lot of work to do. A native speaker, ... (10), hears 'neither' and predicts that 'nor' may come up later in the sentence; .... (11), 'not only' will be followed by 'but also' and 'the more' + adverb will be repeated in a later clause.

Free writing

c Write a paragraph on what you find difficult in language learning and why. Try to use some of the link words from **5a**.

1 Speaking

a   Which of the following diagrams do you think best represents what happens when we read in a foreign language?

A

BEFORE   AFTER

READER

B

MEANING   TEXT

READER

C

MEANING

READER A   READER B

b Match the following statements with the appropriate diagram.
1 The meaning of a text goes straight into the reader's mind.
2 The reader's role is an active one.
3 The reader's role is passive.
4 The reader has to follow instructions carefully.
5 The reader has to struggle to make sense of the text.
6 The reader reconstructs the writer's meaning.
7 The reader just soaks in the writer's meaning.
8 The reader's way is blocked by difficult vocabulary and grammar.

2 Reading Skills

a Read the first and last sentence in the text below and give it a title.

b Look at the complete text and underline all references to lemons.

c How many styles of reading are mentioned?

Developing reading skills involves training ourselves to adopt a number of different reading styles related to our reasons for reading. In fact, it is this ability to switch styles according to purpose which makes for efficient reading. We have to get used to the idea that plodding through a text word by word or squeezing it dry like a lemon until every word is fully understood are not the only ways to approach reading in a foreign language. In fact, if students do take this intensive approach to every text they are likely to feel pretty exhausted and frustrated before long. Let us, therefore, make a basic distinction between intensive reading on the one hand and global reading on the other. The former is the lemon-squeezing approach where every word and structure becomes part of the students' active command of the language, while the latter takes the text as a whole and aims for a general understanding. Thus we may skim a text to get a first impression of its basic meaning, the gist, before we go on to study it more carefully. If we know what we're looking for in a text, we are searching or scanning for a specific piece of information. Having acquired an initial impression of the text, selected the information we want and finally explored the detail (what is sometimes called receptive reading) we respond in some way. The simplest response is to just think about what the writer has said; we may make notes, report what we have read to someone else or discuss it with them. We may call this responsive reading. Our response will depend on what our purpose is in reading, so in developing reading skills in a foreign language it is important to have a reason for reading.

d Find words to complete the following diagram.

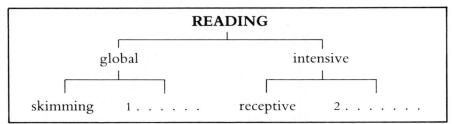

e Do you think the writer would agree with the following statements?
1 There is one style of reading.
2 One style of reading is better than another.
3 We should try to read quickly.
4 We must always skim before we scan.
5 Listening is like reading.

f Look back at exercises **2a–e**. What was the purpose of each exercise in terms of the reading skills described in the text, for example: global, intensive, skimming, scanning, etc.?

Vocabulary

g In the following list of words from the text there are ten pairs of words with the same or nearly the same meaning. Find these pairs.
Example: *understand/comprehend*

basic	ability	skill	idea
understand	simple	therefore	difference
purpose	search	get	initial
scan	thus	distinction	acquire
reason	comprehend	first	impression

3 Reading Using context

a Before you read the text below, write down one characteristic of a good reader.

b Read the text to see if the writer agrees with you. Then answer the questions below.

One mark of a frickled reader is his ability to decide what he can safely ignore. This is something many prudents have renev contemplated; it may seem to them wrong because it is not done in class. Foredown, it needs to be done in class to make it respectable. It may also seem dangerous and it is, which is why it needs to be practised ronder the talkster's guidance.

1 Which words did you find difficult?
2 Are they nouns, verbs, adjectives, adverbs, prepositions . . .?
3 Which words do you think are important/unimportant?

c Can you answer the following questions without knowing what the nonsense words mean?

1 Does the text tell you how to become a good reader?
2 Does the good reader understand every word in a text?
3 Mention one thing that makes a good reader.
4 Is this very common? Why not? (Give two reasons.)
5 Does the writer agree with these reasons?
6 What can be done to overcome this problem?

Conclusion: What does the exercise you have just done demonstrate about reading?

d Which of the nonsense words in the text could mean the same as:

1 with	5 moreover	9 without
2 skilled	6 learners	10 efficient
3 under	7 teacher	11 bad
4 not	8 therefore	12 students

4 Reading Prediction

You are going to read a text which has been split up into individual phrases. First cover the whole of the text apart from the title and Question 1. Answer the question, then uncover the next line and check your prediction. Continue in the same way, uncovering only one line at a time.

TITLE: | **LEONARDO AND HIS TIMES** |

Q1 What kind of information do you expect to find in this text?

| Leonardo lived from 1452 to 1519. |

Q2 What information about Leonardo are we going to be given next?

| He was born near the small town of Vinci, which |

Q3 Which what?

| lies between Pisa and Florence.
His father was a young lawyer. |

Q4 The next sentence will be about his
a) sister? b) brother? c) mother? d) grandfather?

| We cannot be sure who his mother was |

Q5 Which word will probably come next?

| but it is likely she was a village girl. |

Q6 Why don't we know more about Leonardo's mother?

> Leonardo's father did not marry his mother; instead

Q7 What do you think he did instead?

> he married into a good family of Florence.

Q8 Are we going to be told anything about this marriage? What?

> This marriage was childless; only in his last marriage, more than twenty years afterwards,

Q9 Look at the grammar of this last sentence. What is the next word going to be?

> did Leonardo's father have children again. Leonardo was thus

Q10 The writer will now
   a) give an example?
   b) begin a new topic?
   c) describe a result?

> his father's only child all through his childhood and youth.

Q11 Why are we being told all this?

> What did his age think about his illegitimacy?

Q12 What does the question mark tell you about what comes next?

> The answer is that illegitimacy itself was a commonplace.

Q13 Is the next sentence going to be
   a) an example?
   b) a comparison?

> Men were proud of making their own way and indeed

Q14 What do people often do when they are proud?

> many cardinals and well-known artists such as Leon Battista Alberti boasted that

Q15 What?

> they were born out of wedlock. Indeed,

Q16 Will the writer move on to a new topic now?

> these men frequently wielded a power which was as

Q17 The writer will now
   a) give an example?
   b) make a comparison?

> illegitimate as their birth.

5 Writing

Pre-writing

a Complete the following summary of the reading process (the first words of each incomplete sentence are given to help you).

The reasons for reading are essentially practical; that is to say reading is carried out for a purpose. For example, ... (1). Consequently, the student should be less concerned with the language than with the message it communicates. If the reader approaches every text as if it were a test of grammar and vocabulary, ... (2). Thus, different kinds of skills are involved depending on the reading task. On the one hand, ... (3). On the other, we may choose to read fast, particularly when reading for pleasure. We also read fast when .... (4). However, this ability to switch styles when reading is something that has to be taught. The teacher or textbook will have to .... (5). Ultimately, of course, the students themselves will have to develop this skill through exposure to a wide variety of texts.

Free writing

b Now write about the different kinds of reading you do in English and in your own language. How do **you** approach the difficulties of reading in a foreign language?

1 Speaking

Have you written (in English) the following kinds of writing recently? Which do you find useful? Tick (√) those which you find useful, and in groups, discuss the reasons for your answers.

Kind of writing	Useful		Kind of writing	Useful
1 For and against essay	...		9 Dialogue	...
2 Diary	...		10 Lecture notes	...
3 Scientific report	...		11 Postcard	...
4 Letter to a friend	...		12 Letter of complaint	...
5 Descriptive essay	...		13 Grammar exercises	...
6 Application form	...		14 Summary	...
7 Letter requesting information	...		15 Business letter	...
8 Telegram	...		16 Notes taken from a book	...

2 Reading

Appreciating style

a   Match the following extracts of written English with the kinds of writing listed in the table above.

1

GOT HERE AT LAST!
WEATHER'S LOVELY - FOOD GREAT
THE PEOPLE ARE REALLY
FRIENDLY.

2

We have just returned from a holiday in Majorca organized by your travel agency – we were due to return on Monday but in fact got back yesterday – three days later than originally arranged. That is not all.

3

Bennet (1984) called attention to the non-normal distribution of daily global radiation counts based on his analysis of the June and December values for a number of North American cities. Further research in this area was conducted by Dubrovsky (1985).

4

Many people nowadays, particularly adults, claim young people have too much freedom; in the old days the young generation knew how to behave themselves. By this they mean that children respected their parents and obeyed their teachers. They argue that all this has changed: what the young generation needs today is more discipline.

5

Bellomondo, a large seaside resort, is one of the main towns of the region and it is also one of the most beautiful. It has mile upon mile of beaches and has always been popular with tourists. It is a historical town and at the same time a thoroughly modern one. One look at the skyline is enough to establish this.

b The sentences below belong with the extracts you have just read. Match each one with the appropriate extract and say whether it begins or continues the extract.

1 The hotel accommodation provided was way below the standard we were led to expect.
2 The domes and spires of the ancient cathedral reflect the autumn sunlight as do the glinting windows of the towering office-blocks.
3 Having a marvellous time. Wish you were here.
4 There are two ways of looking at this question: on the one hand, from the point of view of the parents and on the other, from the point of view of young people themselves.
5 His findings confirmed those of previous researchers.

c Place the five extracts on the scale below.

Most formal (e.g. legal documents)	Neutral	Most informal (e.g. chatting to friends)
10 -----------------------------------	5	--------------------------------------- 0

d Now continue each of the extracts with an appropriate sentence; read your sentences out to the rest of the class and ask them to guess which of the five they go with.

e Continue passage 4 of **2a** ('Many people nowadays . . .') by putting the following jumbled extracts in the right order.

1 Most young people, on the other hand, believe freedom is the most important thing in life – freedom to enjoy yourself and live your life as you please.

2 It is not difficult then to see why young people reject appeals for more discipline.

3 Parents, of course, see the problem of discipline very differently from their children; for them the most important factor to take into consideration is their children's future career.

4 Furthermore, they are not impressed by what adults have achieved through so-called discipline. The world of adults seems characterized by conflict and compromise.

5 They want their children to be respectable, law-abiding citizens; discipline is therefore necessary as a means to achieving this end. If young people work hard and make sacrifices now, they will be successful and prosperous later on in life.

6 They question the value of planning ahead and prefer to make the most of the present. Discipline for them is something you find at school and in the army.

7 People who talk about discipline are often the same people who argue for corporal punishment and who in the past believed war was necessary for a variety of questionable reasons.

3 Reading / Writing

a The following student's essay contains a lot of mistakes. Read it quickly and suggest a suitable title.

I want to ask what discipline we do mean – the discipline in the army or *aux/a* the discipline in the society, the discipline that everyone is putting on the *a* youth in our days? I go to school with laws and 'don'ts' OI go home and it happens the same. Nobody lets us free to react as free to show our good *w.o.* attitude towards the society. We live in a world full of 'don'ts' – is it fair I *a* think no, we should get more chances to react spontaneously. Well I also think my parents agree up to a certain extent. Though don't forget that *st* schools and other institutes can't depend on your good wish. An you may ? *?* have it other don't. Many people proves in the everyday life that they *ag./a* can't be trusted. On the other hand, I agree that pressure brings some-times, the opposite results from the desired ones.

t I <u>was thinking</u>ᴧthis very subject many timesⅾ think that whatᴧsee out in the

p streets is the result <u>from</u> the hard pressure on⟨schoolkids.⟩ We need to feel   *st*

more free. To\do certain thin🄑s just because we want to <u>try</u> our own

a mistakesₒThe society⟨and⟩the teachers and <u>the</u> parents are so hard on us.

+/a <u>Yes</u>, <u>the</u> society must⟨to⟩protect <u>herself</u>, teachers <u>wants</u> their own⟨pie🄑ce   *ag.*

and mind. That's why <u>need we more freedom no less.</u>   *w.o.*

---

b Match the symbols used by the teacher with their meaning.

Symbol	Meaning
1 P	error in word order
2 a	word missing
3 st	error in use of auxiliary verb
4 ∧	wrong preposition
5 w.o.	wrong use of article
6 aux	wrong word
7 t	style (too formal or informal)
8 ∼	wrong tense

Symbol	Meaning
9 O	meaning unclear, badly organized
10 ⟨ ⟩	wrong link word
11 ⊏	grammatical error
12 ?	error in spelling or punctuation
13 +	error in agreement (concord)
14 —	start a new paragraph
15 ag	omit this word or phrase

c Rewrite the following parts of the essay, correcting the errors. Use the symbols to help you. The first one has been done for you as an example.

1 ✕ I want to ask what discipline we do mean . . . ✕
   ▶ *I would like to ask what we mean by discipline.*
2 ✕ I go home and it happens the same. ✕
3 ✕ Is it fair. I think no, . . . ✕
4 ✕ I was thinking this subject many times . . . ✕
5 ✕ What see out in the streets is the result from . . . ✕
6 ✕ To do certain thinks because we want. ✕
7 ✕ . . . the society must protect herself . . . ✕
8 ✕ . . . need we more freedom no less. ✕

Vocabulary

d Which of the words in column 1 below does the student use correctly? Correct the errors by choosing an appropriate word from column 2.

1	2
1 put on	impose / exert / enforce
2 law	rule / order / regulation
3 happen	take place / occur / appear
4 react	act / behave / respond
5 fair	just / equal / good
6 wish	desire / will / intention
7 try	attempt / make / try out

Text-attack skills

e The student's essay in **3a** is badly connected – it doesn't 'flow'. Add the link words below to appropriate places in the essay.

in fact	one cannot deny	in my opinion
firstly	in other words	in short
for instance	moreover	

4 Writing

a Below is another essay on the topic of discipline. Indicate the errors by the symbols used in the previous essay.

b Compare it to the essay in **3a** and give each a mark out of 10.

c Rewrite one of the essays correctly.

It is generally agreed that youngsters have changed a lot in the past few years. Many factors contribute to this changement. The today's moral values are different from the ones of the past. The standard of living has risen. Young people enjoy their freedom and independence. The structure of the modern society leads them to a new way of life.

Many grown-up believe that the discipline is necessary for young people today. Very often the young accept responsibilities that are difficult to deal with. They feel as if they know everything in life but they lack experience.

What's more they leave their family very early as they desire to learn about life on their own. The more they are employed in a job and get their own living the more gets dispersed the family unit. Their sexual precocity makes them parents at an early age. Being vulnerable to the dangers of the society they become drug addicted and generally speaking persons rejected from the society.

The idea of applying discipline on the young is partially correct. But this discipline must mean different behaviour of the society towards the young. That's all they want: the legislation of the young must become more strict to make them oppose to the idea of criminality. They must like to live with their parents and not leave it. It is necessary that they must learn to face their responsibilities and accept their faults.

In my point of view this discipline means only one thing. The changement of society.

Extension one

a Fill each of the numbered blanks in the following passage with one suitable word.

A good student can be described as one who is not afraid to make . . . . (1) and is willing to experiment with . . . . (2) language. He learns from his mistakes . . . . (3) constantly tries to develop an alternative, effective . . . . (4) strategy. While the bad . . . . (5) relies too much on the teacher, ... (6) good student is actively involved in . . . . (7) learning process and will, for example, ... (8) intelligent guesses about the meaning of . . . . (9) unknown word or, alternatively, ignore it . . . . (10) it does not seem important to the . . . . (11) meaning of the text. Indeed, complete . . . . (12) is rarely essential – understanding the . . . . (13) is often all that is required. The bad student is . . . . (14) to accept the unknown and will . . . . (15) to squeeze the meaning out of . . . . (16) word. As a result, he will feel . . . . (17) and will eventually abandon the . . . . (18) to learn a foreign language. The good student is . . . . (19) and enthusiastic and has a positive . . . . (20) towards the culture of the people who speak the language; he is invariably receptive to new ideas and ways of learning.

b Fill in the blanks by choosing a suitable form of one word from the following lists.

- however   in fact   therefore   similarly   since
- query   inform   confirm   congratulate   confide
- inhibited   eager   passive   responsive   enthusiastic

1 Our teacher is always arriving late. . . . ., I can't remember him once being on time.
2 When he does arrive, he doesn't seem very . . . . to start the lesson – he wastes a lot of time.
3 If he were more . . . . about his job, perhaps the students would also behave differently.
4 . . . . he shows such little interest himself, it's not surprising he gets hardly any response from the class.
5 His behaviour and the students' response . . . . what many people have said about language learning.
6 If the teacher's role is negative, the learner will be . . . . from speaking.
7 I'm not suggesting he should . . . . them warmly every time they get the third conditional right!
8 If anyone has any . . . . at the end of the lesson he says he'll answer them next time.
9 . . . ., 'next time' never comes.
10 Someone should . . . . him of our dissatisfaction with his teaching methods.

c Complete the table below as far as possible.

Noun	Verb	Adjective
1 experiment	experiment	experimental
2 attention	....	....
3 clarification	....	....
4 comprehension	....	....
5 repetition	....	....
6 prediction	....	....
7 distinction	....	....
8 intention	intend	intentional
9	omit	....
10	indicate	....
11	verify	....
12	confide	....
13	confirm	....
14	inform	....
15	acquire	....
16 enthusiasm	enthuse	enthusiastic
17	....	persuasive
18	....	receptive
19	....	familiar
20	....	ignorant

Is this a useful way to record vocabulary? Does your vocabulary notebook look like this?

d Rewrite the following sentences using the words in brackets. Do not alter these words in any way.
Example:
Children today could do with more discipline. (need)
> ▶ *What children need today is more discipline.*
or ▶ *Children today need more discipline.*

1 A good student is not worried about making mistakes. (afraid)
2 A bad student is not, in most cases, active. (rarely)
3 A bad student will not take risks. (neck)
4 A good student wants to do things off her own bat. (keen)
5 She is not totally dependent on the teacher. (rely)
6 Link words will highlight the logical sequence of a text (be emphasized)
7 Your response to a text is related to your reason for reading it. (depends)
8 One mark of a good reader is the ability to decide what she can safely ignore. (characterized)
9 Some unknown words are probably not essential for comprehension. (likely)
10 A major difference between reading and speaking lies in the nature of the audience. (distinguishes)

2
Stop the world

1 Speaking Look at the photograph and discuss the following questions.

1 What kind of place is shown in the background?
2 Where is the person going?
3 How dangerous or difficult is it?
4 How long will it take?

2 Listening

a Listen to the first part of an interview with the person on the windsurfer and find the answers to the questions you discussed.

b In groups, think of questions you would like to ask this person about the voyage and write them in a grid like the one over the page. Then listen to the second part of the interview and note the answers to your questions.

Question	Answer
How did you...	

Locating specific information

🔲 **c** Listen again and note any other questions the interviewer asked, and the answers, in the grid.

🔲 **d** Listen again and work out the meaning of the following phrases.
1 'the old body just complained'
2 'I had a mother ship'
3 'we would take a radio fix'
4 'once I got the idea in my head I couldn't let it go'
5 'I've flirted with the idea of windsurfing round the world'

e Discuss the following questions.

1 Why do you think Tim was concerned about rules set out by the Guinness Book of Records?
2 What do you know about this book?
3 Would you like to get an entry in the book, and if so, what would it be?

3 Grammar Preparatory *it* and *-ing* form

a What did you think of Tim's exploit? You could describe it like this:
He was crazy. He windsurfed 2000 miles around Britain.

We can say the same thing by using a preparatory *it*:
It was crazy of him to windsurf 2000 miles round Britain.

Or we can use the *-ing* form:
Windsurfing 2000 miles round Britain was crazy.

b We could also describe Tim's exploit as:

bold	fearless	absurd
brave	reckless	ridiculous
courageous	mad	

Using both of the patterns in italic above, write four sentences which describe how you feel about his exploit.

c In pairs, make a list of all the problems Tim could have faced on his voyage. Then, using the patterns and adjectives above, exchange opinions with another partner and give reasons.
Example:
It was courageous of him to windsurf round Britain because no one had attempted it before.

4 Reading / Writing

Gist reading

a Match the newspaper articles with the right headlines.

Death Wish 5000

Stunted Boat Stunt

Jumper's French Feat

It's snow risk?

Self-torture reaches new heights

2 Take an ordinary lawn chair, a few balloons filled with helium and what have you got? A quiet afternoon on the beach with the kids? Nothing so conventional! For John Wright it's the thrill of a lifetime as he soars up to 5,000 metres ...

1 The current fad of jumping off very tall buildings arrived in France this week when Scot Ian Mackenzie accepted an incredible challenge from friends in his local and leapt off the Eiffel Tower with a parachute.

5 The alarming race to become the fastest person on skis continued today as a new record of 150 kilometres an hour was set by Texan Ed Walker. This bizarre form of downhill skiing has already claimed one life this week but there are plenty of daredevils lining up to take on Ed ...

4 Most of us have had a fantasy or two about cruising the Caribbean in a 70-footer. Quite an adventure, but not for Bob Jones. Far too humdrum for him. Sailors are normally prudent people but his idea of cruising is crossing the Atlantic in a boat just 2.5 metres long . . .

3 In what some say is the most reckless feat yet, bank clerk Arthur Miller yesterday reached the end of his adventure. Ignoring the safer route to the top, he chose the deadly north face and scaled it alone and without oxygen.

Vocabulary

b Read the headlines and articles again and complete the list of nouns and adjectives used to talk about the exploits.

Nouns	Adjectives
feat	*incredible*
s	d . . . .
s . . . . – t	a . . . .
d . . . . – w	r . . . .
t	c . . . .
f	p . . . .
c	h . . . .

c What do you think of the exploits in the newspaper articles in **4a**? Exchange opinions with your partner using the patterns in **3a** and give your reasons.

d Using the patterns and vocabulary you have practised, write a sentence describing each of the exploits.

e Now think of another crazy stunt someone might do and write a sentence to describe it. How many can you think of?
Example:
Climbing Everest alone, without oxygen, and with one hand tied to your back would be ridiculous.

5 Writing

Pre-writing

a Rewrite the following text adding all necessary punctuation: full stops (.), commas (,), colons (:), semi-colons (;), hyphens (-), exclamation marks (!), question marks (?), CAPITAL LETTERS, and divide the text up into three paragraphs.

amazing feats and breath taking stunts of all sorts have become a craze in recent years flying over a row of cars on a motorbike for instance or sky diving from a plane without a parachute until seconds before its too late such record breaking stunts are now all the rage there are books about them the guinness book of records is a best seller and tv shows like thats incredible are as popular as ever what makes this form of entertainment so popular the answer can be summed up in one word danger danger provides a challenge for the person directly involved in the neck breaking feat while for the spectator it is a thrill albeit a somewhat sadistic one the more frightening the task the better the entertainment the more likely the performer is to break a limb the more fun it is it is the circus tradition extended to a vaster arena life itself people have different opinions about this sort of risk taking whether in the street in the sea or the sky some consider it sport while others regard it as a kind of sado masochism the sceptics ask why cant tight rope walkers always use a net the explanation seems to be that the more dangerous the feat the more pleasure the audience gets out of it and at the same time the performers themselves appear to think it is more skilful balancing without a net personally I think theyre all crazy both those who take such risks and the sadists who pay to watch them

Free writing

b Choose one of the newspaper stories from **4a** and write to the newspaper's editor about it. Include different points of view and conclude with your own opinion of such stunts.

UNIT 6 IT'S ALL RELATIVE

1 Speaking

'A silent man is a dangerous animal.'
Would this be considered true in your country?
Discuss with a partner whether you would keep silent in each of the
following situations. What would it mean in your country if you kept
silent?

1 Meeting strangers
2 Going out with a new boyfriend or girlfriend
3 Seeing your parents again after a period of separation

2 Reading

Gist reading

a Now quickly read these three texts from a book called *Language and
Social Context* and see what the Apache (North American Indian) does in
each situation.

Text 1

'Meeting strangers' (*nda dòhwáá, iltséeda*). The term *nda* labels
categories at two levels of contrast. At the most general level, it desig-
nates any person – Apache or non-Apache – who, prior to an initial
meeting, has never been seen and therefore cannot be identified. In
5   addition, the term is used to refer to Apaches who, though previously
seen and known by some external criterion such as clan affiliation or
personal name, have never been engaged in face-to-face interaction.
In all cases 'strangers' are separated by social distance. And in all cases
it is considered appropriate, when encountering them for the first time,
10 to refrain from speaking.

Text 2

'Courting' (*Líígoláá*). During the initial stages of courtship, young men
and women go without speaking for conspicuous lengths of time.
'Courting' may occur in a wide variety of settings – practically anywhere, in fact – and at virtually any time of the day or night, but
15 it is most readily observable at large public gatherings such as
ceremonials, wakes and rodeos. At these events, *zééde* may stand or
sit (sometimes holding hands) for as long as an hour without exchanging a word. I am told by adult informants that the young people's reluctance to speak may become even more pronounced in situations where
20 they find themselves alone.

Text 3

'Children, coming home'. The Western Apache lexeme *iltá' inatsáá*
is used to describe encounters between an individual who has returned
home after a long absence and his relatives and friends. The most
common type of 'reunion', called *čagáše nakáii*, involves boarding school
25 students and their parents. This type of 'reunion' occurs in late May
or early in June, and its setting is usually a trading post or school, where
parents congregate to await the arrival of buses bringing the children
home. As the latter disembark and locate their parents in the crowd,
one anticipates a flurry of verbal greetings. Typically, however, there
30 are very few or none at all. Indeed, it is not unusual for parents and
child to go without speaking for as long as fifteen minutes.

Vocabulary

b Look through the texts again and find four ways of referring to 'not
speaking'.

c What do you think the following Apache expressions mean?
1 zééde (text 2)
2 iltá inatsáá (text 3)
3 čagáše nakáii (text 3)

Text-attack skills

d Find these words in text 2 and underline them.

Sentence 1   courtship
Sentence 2   courting

Sentence 2   gatherings
Sentence 3   events

Sentence 3   without exchanging a word
Sentence 4   reluctance to speak

Notice how the use of these words 'joins' the text together: *courting* in
sentence 2 refers back to *courtship* in sentence 1; *events* in sentence 3
refers back to *gatherings* in sentence 2.
Now look at text 3 and see if you can find the words that 'join' this text
together in the same way.

e Texts can also be linked by words which point backwards or forwards or
both. Find each of the following (a–e) in the texts in **2a**. Does the word
refer backwards or forwards and what exactly does it refer to?
Example: *In text 1, line 2, 'it' refers back to 'the term nda'.*
a) it (text 1, line 9)
b) them (text 1, line 9)
c) they (text 2, line 20)
d) this (text 3, line 25)
e) the latter (text 3, line 28)

f Underline the linking words or phrases in these sentences. Then place the six sentences in the correct order.

1 Consequently, 'getting cussed out' may involve large numbers of people who are totally innocent of the charges being hurled against them.

2 Although the object of such invective is in most cases the person or persons who provoked it, this is not always the case because an Apache who is truly beside himself with rage is likely to vent his feelings on anyone he sees or who happens to be within range of his voice.

3 They refrain from speech.

4 This lexeme is used to describe any situation in which one individual, angered and enraged, shouts insults and criticisms at another.

5 But whether they are innocent or not, their response to the situation is the same.

6 'Getting cussed out'.

3 Listening

Gist listening

a You are going to hear a lecture on the habits of the Subanun people. There are no posts of authority, such as judge, in Subanun society. Instead, decisions are made at social gatherings. One such gathering is the 'drinking encounter', which is divided into several stages. Listen and write down the stages.

Note-taking

b Listen again and take notes on the characteristics of each stage.

4 Grammar Preparatory *it* clauses

it clauses as preparatory subject

a In the lecture you heard that there are no positions of authority in Subanun society. You might then comment:

| That there are no positions of authority | is odd. |

When the subject of a sentence is a clause, we often prefer to reverse the order above and begin with *it*:

It | *is odd* | *that there are no positions of authority.*

Make the same changes to these sentences.

1	2
1 That there are no judges	is possible
2 How old you are	doesn't matter
3 That they do this	is surprising
4 To drink so much	would worry me
5 For anyone to act as judge	would be thought odd

Now see how many sentences beginning with *it* you can make by matching phrases from the two columns above.

b Using the patterns in **4a**, express your opinion about the Apache Indian from the following prompts.
Example:
to refrain from speaking
▶*It would worry me to refrain from speaking.*

1 to go without talking for long periods
2 for young couples not to talk to one another
3 how long they have known each other
4 that they speak even less when alone
5 not to greet your parents
6 for children to behave like this

it clauses as preparatory object

c Look at this sentence:

The Apaches find │ talking so much in situations like that │ │ odd. │

When the object of a sentence is a clause, we often prefer to change the order and add *it*:

The Apaches find it │ *odd* │ │ *talking so much in situations like that.* │

d Now look at this sentence:

The Apaches consider │ *our* chatting to strangers │ │ unusual. │

Again we prefer to express this using *it*, but in this case we need to change more than the order:

The Apaches consider it │ *unusual* │ │ *that we chat to strangers.* │

Notice that the *it* clause has a different subject ('we') from the main clause ('The Apaches'). Compare with the example in **4c** above.

e Now make similar sentences from the following prompts.
Examples:
I/odd/dance to traditional music at a disco
▶ *I find it odd dancing to traditional music at a disco.*
He/unusual/she/not like this sort of dancing
▶ *He considers it unusual that she does not like this sort of dancing.*

1 I / odd / you / sing in a loud voice in the bath
2 He / unusual / I / get up at 4.30 every morning
3 She / strange / take a cold shower outdoors every day
4 They / odd / she / not spoken to her parents for twenty years
5 We / strange / you / know nothing about the Apaches
6 We / odd / you / never shown any interest in sociology

f Using the patterns in **4b** and **4e**, discuss with your partner the behaviour of people in **your** country that the Apaches and the Subanun would find odd.
Examples:
It would surprise the Subanun how little we drink.
The Apaches would find it strange that young couples talk so much in public.

5 Speaking

If you were one of these people, would you say anything in the following situations? If so, what?
a) a person from your country
b) an English person
c) an Apache
d) an Italian
e) a Scandinavian

1 You meet an old friend who is with two people you have not met before.
2 You are on holiday abroad. On the beach you meet an attractive member of the opposite sex.
3 A friend you made on holiday suddenly arrives at your house six months later.
4 The same friend says some rude things about your country to your parents.

UNIT 7 THAT'S RIDICULOUS!

1 Speaking Look at the following facts about a certain Kirby Groomkirby:

He has hundreds of weighing machines. He is trying to teach them to sing. He then intends to take these weighing machines to the North Pole where their singing will act as a siren to attract thousands of people to the North Pole. Once there he will get them all to jump at the same time. With a bit of luck he hopes this will move the world's axis to one side and this will result in the shifting of the Ice Cap . . .

Can you suggest why Groomkirby should want to do this?
(You should have an answer at the end of the unit.)

2 Listening

Gist listening

▭ **a** Listen to the dialogue and answer the following questions.
1 Where does the scene take place?
2 Who are the speakers?
3 Who are they talking about?
4 What do you think Kirby is accused of?

Locating specific information

▭ **b** Here are some answers spoken by Mrs Groomkirby. What were the questions? Try and guess before you listen again. The first question is given for you as an example.

1 **Q** *You are the mother of the accused, are you not?*
   A I suppose if it's Kirby on trial, I must be.
2 **Q** ....
   A Not really – unless his studies have had anything to do with it.
3 **Q** ....
   A It was an egg-timer to begin with.
4 **Q** ....
   A All his baby things were black.
5 **Q** ....
   A He's an insurance agent, sir.
6 **Q** ....
   A Well, no, sir. Not as far as I know.
7 **Q** ....
   A Well – he has got one or two bottles up in his room.

c 1 Put the following events in the correct order (the first one is done for you).

KIRBY'S EGG-TIMER

a) He rang up NO SALE on the cash register. ☐
b) He rigged up the cash register in the kitchen. ☐ 1
c) He waited for the pips. ☐
d) He waited for four minutes. ☐
e) He put his egg on to boil. ☐
f) He took out the egg. ☐
g) He dialled TIM. ☐
h) He stood there with his stop-watch. ☐

2 How long did this sequence of actions take?
3 Do you think Kirby's egg-timer is ingenious or stupid?

Intonation

d Some of the following statements are really questions. Listen again and tick (√) those that **are** questions.

1 You are Mabel Laurentina Groomkirby.
2 He doesn't feel justified in wearing it except at the funeral of someone he knows.
3 His attitude has changed.
4 He's always been of a very logical turn of mind.
5 He has a cash register, I believe.
6 He likes to have his eggs done the exact time.
7 And so he used the cash register instead.
8 And this was, in fact, the only sequence of actions that took precisely the ten seconds.
9 And he worked this out for himself without any assistance whatever from anyone else.
10 He went to very great trouble indeed.

3 Speaking

Intonation

a Make two questions from each of the following expressions: one should be in the form of a statement and the other an interrogative. Read them aloud. Do both types of sentences sound like questions? (The questions should be based on the dialogue you have heard.)
Example:
the mother of the accused
▶ *You are the mother of the accused?*
▶ *Are you the mother of the accused?*

1 an ingenious young man
2 the only sequence of actions that took ten seconds
3 husband a coloured man
4 negro blood
5 trouble over these jokes

Appreciating style

b 1 Why do both types of question occur in the dialogue you heard?
2 What is the difference between the two types, if any?
3 Who uses the first type of question (the statement with a rising intonation)?

Discussion

c Look back at the facts given about Kirby at the beginning of the unit.
1 Have you guessed the answer to the question?
2 Do you think Kirby is insane? If so, why?

3 Can you give a logical explanation for some of the odd things **you** do? For example, do you do any of the following – if so, can you give a logical explanation for it?
   a) get drunk when it's your birthday or nameday
   b) comb/brush your hair a particular way
   c) wear clothes that match (e.g. why not wear odd socks?)
   d) wear your best clothes on 'special occasions'
   e) wear jackets with buttons on the left/right
   f) say 'good morning' when the weather's awful
   g) say 'I'm fine, thanks' when you're not

4 Reading / Writing

The following summary of what was said at the trial contains numerous errors of fact. How many can you find? Underline the errors, then rewrite the passage correctly.

Mrs Groomkirby said that her son had worn black all his life but that in the last few days he had only felt justified in wearing black at the wedding of someone he knew. She suggested that he had come to think like that as a result of watching too many horror films although he had always been very sensible.

The witness went on to explain the way the egg-timer worked. Once Kirby had rigged up the video and the gas stove, he would put his egg on to boil and after forty minutes he would dial the police, wait for the pips, ring up NO SALE on a cash register and take out the egg. He had worked out this system with his father's help and had later become dependent on it for other things.

When Counsel for the Defence asked Mrs Groomkirby to explain how her son's fondness for black had arisen, she explained that they had planned to dress the baby in white if it had been white, but as he turned out to be black they dressed him in black. She added that her husband, who was an English teacher, was not black. She did not know whether her husband had any negro blood in his room.

She concluded by saying that her son used to give his victims a dictation test before striking them with a hammer. He felt sorry for his victims and went to a great deal of trouble to prepare these tests; above all, he wanted them to end on a sad note – and giving them dictation was the best way to achieve this.

1 Speaking

1 What are the people in the photographs below doing?
2 Do these stunts serve a useful purpose?
3 What do you think of such stunts?
4 Have you ever done anything like this? Would you do so if you could?
5 If you were a journalist, which of these events would you choose to write about? Why?

2 Reading / Listening

Discussion

a Write down three headlines for surprising events you have read about in the newspapers recently (if you can't remember the actual headlines, make up your own).

b Discuss whether your headlines refer to good or bad news and why.

Locating specific information

c In pairs, each read one of the two lists of headlines opposite. Find any items similar to the ones you wrote in **2a** above.

A	B
1 Rock star to buy Greek island	1 Tiny island republic invades US
2 Lone sailor crosses Atlantic in raft	2 UK jobless total tops ten
3 Rembrandt sold for £1 million	3 Whale now extinct
4 US invades tiny Caribbean island	4 Dolphin understands English says trainer
5 Brain transplant a success says surgeon	5 Millions homeless – UN report
6 US astronauts land on Mars	6 Jealous husband bites poodle
7 Extra-terrestrial captured by children	7 Soccer defeat sparks revolution in Salvador
8 Cancer increase – smoking to blame	8 Hollywood star new US president
9 Accidental nuclear war possible – says expert	9 China lifts ban on Beethoven
10 Palestinian–Israeli peace signed	10 Everest conquered without oxygen
11 Computer games for all the family	11 Tobacco sales up
12 Ping-pong hooliganism on the increase	12 Boeings collide in mid-air
13 China lifts ban on Shakespeare	13 Millionaire to buy Parthenon
14 Agatha Christie awarded Nobel prize	14 Government to abolish income tax
15 Whale faces extinction	15 US welcomes UK to union
16 UK to be new US state	16 Libya to be new member of EEC
17 Unemployed in Britain over 4 million	17 Nuclear war by computer threat
18 Chimpanzee plays Mozart sonata	18 Computer new director of multi-national
19 Watch-size TV arrives	19 Soviet cosmonauts land on Venus
20 More missiles in Europe soon	20 Titian's 'Death of Actaeon' bought for £20

Gist listening

 d Now listen to the news broadcast and, looking at only your own list of headlines, note which news items are mentioned in the broadcast. Then exchange information with your partner.

3 Speaking

Do we live in a crazy world? Read your headlines again.

1 Which do you think are fact and which are fantasy?
2 Which of the 'fantasy' headlines do you think might happen in the future?
3 Which headlines make you think that it **is** a crazy world?

In groups of As and Bs exchange views. Explain to members of the group the reasons for your answers.

4 Writing

Pre-writing

a Look at the following notes and read the two texts below. Decide which writer (A or B) might use each of these notes (you may decide that some of them might be used by both writers).

		A	B
1	threat of nuclear destruction	☐	☐
2	famine in third world countries	☐	☐
3	videos available to all	☐	☐
4	violence amongst young people	☐	☐
5	free speech, more democracy	☐	☐
6	increase in use of drugs	☐	☐
7	the relationship between the sexes	☐	☐
8	'modern' diseases on the increase	☐	☐
9	many diseases now rare	☐	☐
10	more government control over our lives	☐	☐
11	parents have less control over their children	☐	☐
12	the use of computers in everyday life	☐	☐

(A)

There is far too much pessimism about nowadays - all people do is moan, moan, moan. In my view this is completely unfounded. People should look around them to see what a wonderful world this is, what a glorious life they lead. All around us there are signs of progress and of co-operation between people and nations.

Only a century ago millions were homeless and were lucky if they got one square meal a day. Most children - and women - were illiterate and worked like slaves for the mere right to live. Today, we all live in relative comfort, protected from disease and natural disasters. Yes, indeed, we've never had it so good. If only we knew it.

What a mess the world is in today – whatever has humanity done to deserve such a fate? So much potential wasted, so much knowledge used to evil ends. Half the world living in the lap of luxury and the other half on the point of starvation. In the so-called developed countries students protest about how bad their university education is while in the rest of the world they don't even have schools. Technology has become a nightmare of imminent destruction. We are surrounded by sophisticated gadgets but cannot walk the streets safely at night. While a few have all the wealth, millions are unemployed.

Free writing

b In **4a** above you looked at texts in which the writer put only one side of the argument – so that while one text was clearly optimistic, the other was definitely pessimistic. However, often in essays or written discussions you are expected to make arguments both 'for' and 'against' before reaching a conclusion.

Points to remember

Overall plan – it is useful to organize your writing into paragraphs. For instance, in this case you might use the following plan:

Introduction
Arguments 'for'
Arguments 'against'
Conclusion

Link words – you will need to compare and contrast different points of view. For this purpose it is useful to include some of the following link words:

Adding information		Contrasting information	
Similarly,		*However,*	
In the same way,	+ **clause**	*Nevertheless,*	+ **clause**
Likewise,		*In contrast,*	
Moreover,		*On the other hand,*	

Here are some examples:
Terrorism is on the increase; **similarly,** *there are more armed robberies than there used to be.*
We are now more informed than we used to be; **however,** *a lot of information is still unavailable to the public.*
We should be building more schools; **likewise,** *more should be spent on hospitals ...*
Nuclear power stations have increased in number; **in contrast,** *the number of coal mines has dropped.*

Now write an essay on the following statement from a Lennon/McCartney song: 'Things are getting better all the time'. Base your essay on the notes in **4a** if you want.

Extension two

a   Fill each of the numbered blanks with one suitable word.

What sort of a world is this we live in? In some countries people spend months on court cases costing millions. In other places there are .... (1) positions or offices of authority, and arguments are settled, literally, over a drink. .... (2) sort of approach would itself lead to arguments in many countries. Imagine basing a decision .... (3) verbal artistry, and imposing a .... (4) as a consequence! Some, of course, would say that .... (5) artistry is exactly what wins court cases, and therefore the former system is no better than the .... (6).

Most of us are too prudent to perform a .... (7) like jumping off the Eiffel Tower without a parachute. But should we consider those who do such things .... (8) just because we are not .... (9) enough to have a go? Should we criticize the .... (10) who are willing? Perhaps we had better .... (11) from criticism. Where, after all, do you draw the line between an .... (12) holiday and a dangerous .... (13)?

In some places it would be considered .... (14) to speak on certain occasions, whereas in our country we would not hesitate to do .... (15). We might well .... (16) it strange that parents and children have .... (17) reunions but others may find such a thing perfectly .... (18). All in all, it is difficult to judge such encounters and events and however .... (19) we find them, it is perhaps better to avoid using words .... (20) 'crazy'.

b   Choose the word which best completes each sentence.

1   She is absolutely .... about dancing.
     a) exciting   b) crazy   c) reckless   d) bizarre
2   You have to be pretty .... to want to climb Everest.
     a) adventurous   b) risky   c) provoked   d) challenging
3   He's really .... in his opinions about marriage – he just wants to meet someone to settle down with.
     a) intrepid   b) prudent   c) conventional   d) bold
4   She saw a really .... horror film last night.
     a) reckless   b) fearless   c) scary   d) dangerous
5   He took a/an .... risk when he dived from the cliff into the sea.
     a) evaluated   b) educated   c) logical   d) calculated
6   His sailing the Atlantic in a raft was a remarkable ....
     a) ability   b) achievement   c) attribute   d) struggle
7   The Government is the highest .... in the country.
     a) authority   b) position   c) office   d) accomplishment
8   The pilot performed a few clever .... before he landed his plane.
     a) feats   b) risks   c) performance   d) stunts
9   She has an .... mind – she ought to become an inventor.
     a) intrepid   b) ingenious   c) illogical   d) innocent
10 After a great .... he managed to swim back to the shore.
     a) challenge   b) competition   c) struggle   d) exploit

c Complete the table below as far as possible, checking your answers with a dictionary. Note any change of meaning from one part of speech to another.
Example:
calculation/calculate means 'working out/to work something out' but *calculating* can also mean 'deceitful'.

Noun	Verb	Adjective
1 calculation	calculate	*calculating*
2 extension	extend	. . . .
3	. . . .	exciting
4	impress	. . . .
5	remark	. . . .
6	notice	. . . .
7 observation	. . . .	. . . .
8	risk	. . . .
9	. . . .	accomplished
10 authority	. . . .	. . . .
11 emotion	. . . .	. . . .
12	invite	. . . .
13 origin	. . . .	. . . .
14	continue	. . . .
15 person	. . . .	. . . .

d Rewrite the following sentences, beginning with the words given.
1 That there are only twenty-eight days in February is odd.
It . . .
2 It does not matter how tall you are.
How . . .
3 Climbing Everest without oxygen was courageous of her.
It . . .
4 I would be worried if I smoked so much.
It . . .
5 It is crazy to try to teach weighing machines to sing.
Trying . . .
6 The journey round Britain took him seventy days.
It . . .
7 He couldn't think of anything else except windsurfing round Britain.
The only . . .
8 What makes this form of entertainment so popular is danger.
It . . .
9 It is not unusual for parents and child to go without speaking for fifteen minutes.
For . . .
10 Kirby doesn't wear black except at the funeral of someone he knows.
It is only . . .

3
Me and the animals

1 Reading / Writing

Prediction

a Look at this headline. What do you think it is referring to?

BACK FROM THE DEAD

Gist reading

b Now read the text below quickly. Find the answer to **1a**. Find out what
the WWF does.
What do you think WWF stands for?

Eagles, falcons, buzzards, kites and condors have become threatened. Their decline has been accelerated by the destruction of their feeding and nesting places: by the collection of eggs, and above all by pesticides which enter their food chains leading to sterility and malformation of young and mass deaths. A captive breeding programme for the peregrine falcon in the United States aided by the WWF is now raising 100 birds a year. Also, with WWF backing, several European countries are co-operating to save the white-tailed sea eagle. Nests have been guarded and breeding has improved following the provision of uncontaminated food at crucial periods in the breeding cycle.

Perhaps the WWF's most successful effort has been the conservation of the polar bear. Its survival was threatened by hunters using rifles, motorboats and aircraft among the ice floes of the Arctic, and by disturbance of its habitat. The WWF helped bring polar bear specialists together to co-ordinate research and protection. As a result, the five circumpolar nations — Norway, Canada, the Soviet Union, the USA and Denmark — have signed an agreement to ban killing of the polar bear, except by local Eskimos who depend on it for survival. Denmark has established the Northeast Greenland National Park, largest in the world, which protects important denning areas of the polar bear. Norway has created polar bear reserves in the Svalbard archipelago.

The Arabian oryx, a creamy white antelope with long graceful horns, had been hunted almost to extinction. The Fauna Preservation Society, with WWF help, mounted an expedition to capture a few of the last thirty and ship them to the Phoenix Zoo in Arizona. There, through captive breeding, they have become the nucleus of a world herd.

Note-taking

c Look at the text again and complete the table below.

	Problem	Solution		Problem	Solution
White-tailed sea eagle			Polar bear		
Peregrine falcon			Arabian oryx		

Vocabulary

d Here are some words from the text in **1b**. Put them in the table below, then complete the table where possible. Notice that the same word may fit in more than one column (for example *ban*).

threat   nest   extinct   conservation
extinction   breeding   protect   captive
decline   destroy   establishment   breed
hunt   conserve   *ban*   nesting
reserve   survive   habitat   destruction
acceleration   *threaten*   survival   accelerate

Noun	Verb	Adjective
threat	*threaten*	*threatening*
ban	*ban*	*banned*

Now use a dictionary to check your answers.

e Match the words in column A below with the definitions in B. Note that there is one word for which there is no definition.

A	B
1 thrive	a) care for and protect land and animals
2 become extinct	b) give something (e.g. money) to charity
3 donate	c) keep from change or destruction
4 contribute	d) kill animals in large numbers
5 conserve	e) join with others in giving help, money, etc. to a common cause
6 slaughter	f) die out, no longer exist
7 preserve	g) grow strong and healthy, develop
8 fund	

2 Grammar   Written reports

a   Look at the first paragraph of the text in **1b**. How many passive verbs are there?

b   In newspaper articles or reports like the one in **1b**, it is common to use noun phrases to describe events. Compare the following sentences from the text with the way someone might say the same thing.

Text version	**Spoken version**
Their decline has been accelerated by . . .	Numbers are declining and the situation has been accelerated because . . .
. . . *the destruction of* their *feeding* and *nesting* places.	. . . the places where they feed and nest have been destroyed.

Now rewrite the following sentences using the noun phrases given.

1   The marine life in some areas is declining and this is one of the WWF's major concerns.
  The decline of . . .
2   The survival of certain bird species was threatened but this has been overcome as a result of the WWF's campaign.
  The threat to . . .
3   The areas where they breed are now safe.
  . . . breeding areas . . .
4   Hunting the polar bear has been banned and this has encouraged hope for its survival.
  The ban on . . .
5   A Danish National Park protects the areas where the polar bear makes its dens.
  . . . denning areas . . .
6   Sea eagles' nests have been protected and this has helped save the species.
  The protection of . . .

c   The article in **1b** is concerned with the solutions to certain conservation problems and the results of those solutions. Complete the sentences below as if you were writing an article about the results of the WWF's activities. Use information from the text, and the passive and/or noun phrases where you can.
  Example:
  As a result of a captive breeding programme a hundred peregrine falcons are now raised each year.

1   As a result of the campaign by the WWF . . .
2   Thanks to . . .
3   Following the efforts of the WWF . . .
4   With support from the WWF . . .
5   Aided by . . .
6   Through . . .

3 Listening

Inference

📼 **a** Someone is collecting money on behalf of the WWF. Listen to the three people she calls on, and decide which one is most likely to give money.

Note-taking

📼 **b** Listen again and note down what is said about each of the following. Some notes are given to help you.

5,000, Operation Tiger, reserves, conservation projects, women embarrassed, fashion magazines, export bans, controls on importation,

50, Wildfowl Trust, 700, captive pairs, 200, Hawaii, natural habitat,

seas, whales, turtles, slaughtered, handbags, ivory, bludgeoned to death, threat of extinction, sanctuaries, nesting sites

4 Writing

Using the notes you made in **3b** write an advertisement for the WWF. Use vocabulary from **1e** and lay the advertisement out like this:

Headline: (Choose your own.)
Paragraph 1:
The World Wildlife Fund was formed to . . . . Here is an outline of some of the things we have achieved so far.
Paragraph 2:
(Use your notes from the listening passages.)
Paragraph 3:
The World Wildlife Fund needs to meet the increasing demands for . . . . as the requirement for conservation action becomes more varied and most urgent. It needs continuing . . . . . ., not only . . . . but also moral, from everyone who believes in the . . . . of nature for the future generations. . . . . projects throughout the world need much more money than the World Wildlife Fund has available. Please find out how you can . . . . by writing to:

WWF International
Membership Secretary
World Conservation Centre
1196 Gland, Switzerland

WWF

1 Reading / Speaking

a In this unit we shall be looking at extracts from *Animal Farm* by George Orwell. Here is the 'blurb' from the cover of the Penguin Edition of *Animal Farm*. Fill each of the numbered blanks in the text with one suitable word.

George Orwell

Animal Farm

In this biting satire upon dictatorship, George Orwell makes use of the technique perfected by Swift in *A Tale of a Tub.* It is the history of a revolution which went . . . . (1), and of the excellent excuses . . . . (2) were forthcoming at every step for each perversion of the original doctrine. The animals on a farm drive . . . . (3) their master and take . . . . (4) the farm for themselves. The experiment is . . . . (5) successful, except for the unfortunate fact that someone has to take the deposed farmer's place. Leadership devolves almost automatically upon the pigs, ... (6) are on a higher intellectual plane than the rest of the animals. Unhappily their character is not equal to their intelligence and out of this fact springs the main development of the story. The last chapter brings a dramatic change, ... (7) as soon as it has happened is seen to have been inevitable from the start.

b After the animals' rebellion the human beings return to capture the farm. The extract below describes the battle that follows. Read the text and where a choice of words is given, choose the one you feel sounds more vivid.

THE BATTLE
OF
THE COWSHED

starring

Snowball, the pig
Muriel, the goat
Benjamin, the donkey
Boxer, the horse

and, of course, the pigeons, geese, sheep, cows, the cat and the rest of the pigs and horses . . .

As the human beings approached the farm buildings Snowball launched his first attack. All the pigeons flew to and fro over the men's heads and muted upon them from mid-air; and while the men were dealing with this, the geese, who had been hiding behind the hedge (*ran out/rushed out*) and (*bit/pecked*) viciously at the calves of their legs. However, this was only a light skirmishing manoeuvre, intended to create a little disorder, and the men easily drove the geese off with their sticks.

Snowball now launched his second line of attack. Muriel, Benjamin and all the sheep, with Snowball at the head of them (*ran/rushed*) forward and (*prodded/pushed*) and (*struck/butted*) the men from every side, while Benjamin turned round and (*hit/lashed*) at them with his small hoofs. But once again the men, with their sticks and their hobnailed boots, were too strong for them; and suddenly, at a (*squeal/shout*) from Snowball which was the signal for retreat, all the animals turned and (*ran/fled*) through the gateway into the yard.

Inference

c 1 Who is the leading figure at this point in the story? Underline all the expressions which lead you to form this impression.

2 Which side is winning the battle so far? Why?

Prediction

d The following extracts are from the next part of the story and are in the correct order. Discuss who you think the pronouns refer to and how the battle will continue.

The men gave a shout of triumph. . . . Jones . . . raised his gun and fired. . . . Panic overtook them . . . . . . he yelled horribly. . . . they were in . . . retreat . . .

2 Listening

Gist listening

a You will hear the next part of the story of *Animal Farm*. Listen and put the pictures below in the correct order (the first one has been done for you).

Boxer . . . . on his hind legs and . . . . with his hoofs.

Jones was . . . . into a pile of . . . .

The men . . . . after their enemies in disorder.

The men in retreat with a flock of geese . . . . after them.

1 Snowball . . . . the signal for the . . . .

The cat . . . . her claws in the cowman's neck.

Locating specific information

b Look back at **1d** – were you right about the extracts?

c Listen again and complete the captions below each picture.

Vocabulary

d Complete the table below by putting each of the following words under the heading which gives its general meaning. Use your dictionary to help you.

butt	lash	fling	rush
sink	squeal	gore	dash
rear up	fly	prod	hiss

	General Meaning					
	'move quickly'	'hit or push'	'move higher'	'move lower'	'make a noise'	'throw'
Example	leap	strike peck	raise	drop	yell	hurl

e In pairs, complete the following summary of the text using the verbs in the table in **2d** in the past tense. Student A should complete numbers 1–13 and student B numbers 14–25.

A

1 The men *gave* a shout of triumph.
2 The men . . . . after their enemies.
3 Some animals *emerged* in their rear.
4 These animals *cut* the men off.
5 Snowball *gave* the signal for the charge.
6 Snowball . . . . straight for Jones.
7 Jones *saw* him coming.
8 Jones . . . . his gun.
9 Jones *fired* his gun.
10 A sheep . . . . dead.
11 Snowball . . . . his fifteen stone against Jones's legs.
12 Jones was . . . . into a pile of dung.
13 The gun . . . . out of Jones's hand.

B

14 Boxer . . . . on his hind legs.
15 Boxer . . . . out with his iron-shod hoofs.
16 The blow *stretched* a stable-lad lifeless in the mud.
17 Panic *overtook* the men.
18 The animals *chased* the men.
19 The animals *gored* the men.
20 The cat . . . . off the roof.
21 The cat . . . . her claws in the cowman's neck.
22 The man . . . . horribly.
23 The men . . . . out of the yard.
24 The geese . . . . after them.
25 The geese *pecked* at their calves.

Now tell your partner your part of the story so that you both have the 25 completed sentences.

3 Writing

Appreciating style

a   Orwell criticized many English writers for writing bad English; read what
he says in the following passage and then look back over extracts from
Animal Farm and say whether he practises what he preaches.

'Two qualities are common to all bad writing. The first is staleness of
imagery and the other is lack of precision. The writer either has a meaning
and cannot express it . . . or he is almost indifferent as to whether his words
mean anything or not . . .'

He goes on to give the following 'rules':
a) Never use a metaphor, simile or other figure of speech which you are
used to seeing in print.
b) Never use a long word where a short one will do.
c) If it is possible to cut a word out, always cut it out.
d) Never use a foreign phrase, a scientific word or a jargon word if you can
think of an everyday English equivalent.

1   Do you as a student of English agree with these 'rules'?
2   Does Orwell himself stick to them?
3   Do you think they apply as much to a student of English as they do to a
native speaker?

Summarizing

b   Write a summary of the listening passage using your 25 sentences.
1   Avoid repetition of the same subject by using pronouns like *he, she,
they, it.*
2   Make the text 'flow' by
● adding link words and adverbs of sequence, for example: *soon, as,
then, next, as soon as, suddenly, the next moment, while, after a
moment, a minute later . . .*
● combining two sentences, using *-ing* clauses or clauses beginning
with *as.*
Example:
The men gave a shout of triumph **as they** *rushed after their enemies.*
Suddenly *some animals emerged in their rear,* **cutting** *them off . . .*

c   Write a summary of or a 'blurb' (see **1a**) for a book you have read.

UNIT 11 YOU AND THE ANIMALS

1 Reading / Speaking

Vocabulary

a In pairs, look at the following descriptions of animals, then match the illustrations below with the appropriate descriptions.

1 Small European animal with a pointed nose and bushy tail; it catches rats and rabbits by going into their holes.
2 Small animal, usually brownish-green, that lives in water and on land; it does not have a tail.
3 Long-tailed rodent, similar to but larger than a mouse.
4 Small brown animal that eats other animals; it is slender and has a long tail which is black at the tip.
5 Night bird with large eyes.
6 Flying, mouse-like animal that is active at night.
7 Very large animal that lives in the sea; its blood does not change temperature.
8 Small two-winged fly that stings; it has long, delicate legs and narrow wings.
9 An insect that flies and stings and is usually coloured yellow and black.

Key: a = bee, b = gnat, c = owl, d = stoat, e = bat, f = frog, g = rat, h = ferret, i = whale

b Fill in the blanks in the following sayings and idiomatic expressions using one of these words:

snake   bat   owl
rat   goat   fish
ferret   whale

1 He's as blind as a . . . .
2 She's as wise as an . . . .
3 Behave yourself! Stop acting the . . . .
4 It's great here! We're having a . . . . of a time.
5 He's always drunk; he drinks like a . . . .
6 I've been . . . . . . .ing around all day looking for my watch, but I can't find it anywhere.
7 It must be pouring with rain – you look like a drowned . . . .
8 You can't trust him, despite what he says; he's a . . . . in the grass.

2 Speaking

a In groups, discuss what score (out of 3) you would give each animal for the features given in the table below (0 = terrible, 3 = excellent).

ANIMAL / FEATURE	Cat	Rat	Owl	Dog	Goat	Fish	Whale	Gnat	Frog	Sheep	Human
sight											
hearing											
sense of smell											
speed											
intelligence											
chance of survival											
appearance											
sex life											
Total											

b Compare your results. Which animal scored highest? Which animal scored lowest?

3 Listening / Reading

Prediction

 a   You will hear a poem called 'Me and the Animals' by David Holbrook. Before you listen to the poem, try to fill in the blanks in the text below, paying attention to words that rhyme (for example, *gnat/rat*). Then compare your answers with what you hear.

> ## ME AND THE ANIMALS
>
> 1   I share my kneebones with the gnat,
>   My joints with ferrets, eyes with rat
>   Or blind bat, blinking owl, the goat
>   His golden cloven orb. I mate like a ....
> 5   Or like the heavy whale, that moves a sea
>   To make a mother's gross fecundity.
>
>   I share lung's action with the ....;
>   The fish is cold, but vertebrate like me; my steak
>   Is muscle from a butcher's arm, a butcher's heart
> 10 Is some sheep's breast that throbbed; I ....
>   At noise with ears which in a dog
>   Can hear what I cannot; in water I'm a ....
>
>   I differ most in lacking their content
>   To be, no more. They're at the mercy of the ....,
> 15 Of hot, cold, summer, winter, hunger, anger,
>   Or ritual establishing the herd, smelling out the ....:
>   I walk upright, alone, ungoverned, free:
>   Yet their occasional lust, fear, unease, walk with me
>   Always. All ....

Vocabulary

b   In poetry a word often has more than one meaning. Use your dictionary to find possible meanings for the following words. Which is the most appropriate meaning in the context of the poem?

1 joint	4 orb	7 fecundity	10 content
2 blinking	5 mate	8 throb	11 scent
3 cloven	6 gross	9 start	12 ritual

Inference

c In pairs or groups, discuss the following.
1 Which of the features in the table in **2a** are mentioned in the poem?
2 Do you think the similarities between the poet and the other animals are flattering to the poet?
3 How many differences between the poet and the animals are mentioned in the text?
4 'yet' (line 18) can be replaced in this context by:
a) nevertheless b) thus c) however d) consequently e) but
5 What is the difference in meaning between 'Always' and 'All ways' (line 19)?
6 Do you think the poet envies the animals? Give reasons for your answer.
7 If you were going to write a poem called 'Me and the Animals', which animals would you write about?

Pronunciation

d Say whether the vowels underlined in the groups of words below sound the same or different. Tick those which are the same (one has been done for you).

A	B	C	A	B	C
gnat	rat	what	√	√	×
goat	owl	stoat			
hear	ear	fear			
golden	cold	cloven			
blind	winter	blink			
hunger	butcher	summer			
anger	stranger	walk			
upright	ungoverned	unease			
snake	make	steak			
lung	lust	muscle			
nature	future	mature			
behind	lined	blind			

4 Reading / Writing

a 1 The following is the first stanza of a poem whose title is the name of an animal. Is it a mouse, giraffe, gorilla or kangaroo?

If the expression on a face	*a*
Means anything, then surely mine	*b*
A member of the human race	*a*
And his, who did not become a man,	*c*
Tell that surpassing must take place	*a*
For what remains to fructify.*	*d*
He has achieved far more than I.	*d*

2 Notice the rhyme scheme of the poem: *face/race/place* and *fructify/I*. Fill in the blanks in the second stanza of the poem bearing in mind the rhyme scheme. Choose from the following words: *conceived, behind, received, outlined, trace, blind, make*

He is himself, now left . . . .
He cannot talk, feel shame or . . . .
Comparisons, but not being . . . .
To his identity, can . . . .
Where his own shadow is . . . .
He passed on what he had . . . .
Until the first man was . . . .

3 Now make one more stanza like the ones above, using the following unpunctuated text. Pay special attention to words that rhyme as these will tell you where some of the lines end. Include CAPITAL LETTERS, full stops (.), commas (,), colons (:), and semi-colons (;).

and is forever what I see faithful to his experience and yet my human fantasy imagines in him wrath at more than being trapped involuntary anger at his successors' dullness who do not understand his wholeness

Free writing

b Now write a composition or a poem called 'A Day in the Life of . . .' about an animal. Don't give the name of the animal – can the rest of the class guess which animal it is?

* to (cause to) produce fruit/successful results

UNIT 12 MY FAMILY AND OTHER ANIMALS

1 Speaking

Look at the illustration and discuss which of the following statements might refer to it.

1 Humans are exploited by animals.
2 Animals should not be kept in cages.
3 Animals are used for research purposes.
4 Animals are exploited by humans.

Which of the captions below matches the statement you chose above?

a) 'Cheese again.'
b) 'This human is well trained – every time I press this switch, he feeds me.'
c) 'I just hate this food you get from machines.'
d) 'Pass the salt, will you?'

Do you agree with the statements?

2 Reading

Gist reading

Look at these statements, and then read the two letters below. Decide which statements go with which letter (A or B). Some may go with both; some may go with neither.

1 Animals are treated fairly.
2 Animals are used in scientific experiments.
3 Live animals should not be used in research.
4 Man is entitled to experiment on animals because of his superior intelligence.
5 Animals should be treated fairly.
6 Living things in less fortunate positions should be looked after.
7 Animals should not be slaughtered for scientific purposes.
8 Pain is inflicted on animals during experiments.

Letter A

Dear Sir,
Many people are concerned with the plight of animals used for research purposes. The offence committed against these animals is not the taking of their lives, it is the pain inflicted upon them. Scientific advancement and humaneness towards animals are compatible. Ethical guidelines have been established for the use of laboratory animals. Live animals should be used only when no adequate alternative exists. Even then, every effort should be made to eliminate suffering.

Letter B

Dear Sir,
It is well known that all sorts of experiments are performed on animals in the name of science. Such experiments are considered to be essential. By possessing a higher intelligence, the human species not only ascends over animals but has a responsibility for them. Basic to the animal rights movement is the belief that those creatures placed in our care by nature must be treated fairly. If this obligation is not fulfilled then we have sunk very low.

3 Listening

Locating specific information

 Listen to this extract from a radio programme concerning listeners' letters. Complete the statements below to match the listeners' opinions.

Mr G Randall

Rare species .... (1) saved from extinction at great cost. Yet animals are .... (2) in laboratories in large numbers. Pain .... (3) inflicted in such animal experiments unless necessary. But the question is not .... (4) but .... (5) itself. Should life .... (6) in some areas but .... (7) in others?

Ms E Sharp

There are many forms of animal .... (8). .... (9) pets be allowed? .... (10) children be taken to the circus? .... (11) horse-riding be permitted? Blood sports should .... (12) be banned. The balance of nature .... (13) preserved by hunting. Human life is .... (14) important than animal life.

4 Grammar *should* + passive

a   When asking people for their views on our responsibilities towards animals you could say:

Do you $\left\{ \begin{array}{l} \text{think} \\ \text{feel} \\ \text{believe} \end{array} \right\}$ *(that) blood sports should be banned?*

Questions like these can be answered briefly in two ways:
Yes, I do/No, I don't.
Yes, they should be/No, they shouldn't be.

In pairs, take it in turns to ask questions and give short answers. Use the following prompts for your questions.
1 live animals/used in experiments
2 animals/treated with respect
3 pain/inflicted on animals
4 rare species/saved from extinction
5 large sums of money/spent on conservation
6 hunting/stopped
7 wildlife/preserved
8 the seas/safeguarded

b   1 Now make up a questionnaire to find out what your class feels about animal rights. You can use the questions you formulated in **4a** as the basis of the questionnaire and add extra questions of your own.

2 In different pairs from the previous exercise, take it in turns to interview each other. The interviewee should give a short answer and reason(s) for that answer.

3 Look at the answers with your partner. Are there any contradictions?

4 Compare your answers with the rest of your class. How does your class feel about our responsibilities to animals?

5 Speaking

'What is the correct relationship between human beings and animals?'
On your own, note down your ideas on the following points.

rare species of animals   nature reserves   animals as pets
polluted seas   animals in circuses   blood sports   starving children
the balance of nature   superiority and responsibility
human tribes in danger of extinction   the cruelty of nature
science and progress

In groups, discuss your ideas.

6 Writing

Pre-writing

a Working in pairs, sort out the sentences below to make two letters to a magazine or newspaper in the debate on animal rights. Both letters express strong views about animal experiments. Writer A is in favour of, Writer B is against such experiments. First mark each sentence 'A' or 'B' depending on whether it is 'for' or 'against'. Then number the sentences to give the correct order (the first two of each letter are done for you).

1 Your correspondents claim to be concerned at the way we treat animals. (B1)

2 I consider there is no alternative to using animals in scientific research. (A2)

3 The pain inflicted on animals for this type of research is unavoidable.

4 Yet one of them considers killing animals is not an offence. (B2)

5 Indeed, it's the price we pay for scientific progress.

6 In conclusion, animal experiments are essential if we want to eliminate disease.

7 First, I believe there should be a total ban on the exploitation of live animals for experimental purposes.

8 To sum up, inflicting pain on animals is certainly not the only way.

9 What kind of concern is this? Isn't killing animals an offence?

10 I feel I must add my views to the debate on the rights of animals. (A1)

11 To halt this progress by banning the use of animals in scientific experiments would be short-sighted and naive.

12 Another correspondent suggests that we have a duty to treat animals fairly.

13 The only way to find a cure for these children is to experiment.

14 Then scientists could concentrate on the many other ways of reducing disease.

15 Yes, we do have such a duty and the only way to do it is to leave animals alone; there *is* an alternative to using animals in scientific research.

16 Those who propose such a ban are forgetting that thousands of children die of incurable diseases each year.

Free writing

b Choose one of the above letters as the basis for a letter to a magazine or newspaper expressing your views on this debate. Make changes where necessary and add any points of your own.

Extension three

a Fill each of the numbered blanks with one suitable word.

Conserving wetlands around the world

.... (1) support and funding, the World Wildlife Fund has helped
.... (2) reserves or protect wetlands in many parts of the world. In the
United States, a substantial purchase of tidal salt marshes along the New
Jersey coast .... (3) helped preserve the .... (4), wintering, and
feeding grounds of more .... (5) 300 bird species. In Britain, the World
Wildlife Fund provided .... (6) for the purchase of Caerlaverock
Wildfowl Reserve – a winter feeding place .... (7) barnacle geese. In
Austria, the World Wildlife Fund took over .... (8) lease of hunting
rights to help establish a reserve in the Seewinkel–Neusiedler Lake area
and also purchased a further reserve in the Marchauen–Marchegg estate,
.... (9) woodland area rich in plant life. In France, the vast wilderness
of the Camargue in the Rhône delta, with its white horses, black bulls and
nesting flamingoes, ... (10) threatened .... (11) commercial
interests. WWF raised .... (12) to consolidate the Camargue as the
basis for a regional .... (13). The Waddenzee wetlands along the
coasts of the Netherlands, West Germany and Denmark, a breeding,
.... (14) and feeding place for five million birds as well as a nursery for
North Sea fish, continue to .... (15) protected with the World Wildlife
Fund .... (16). Denmark has established the north-east Greenland
National Park, largest .... (17) the world, which .... (18)
important denning areas of the polar bear. Norway has .... (19) polar
bear reserves in the Svalbard archipelago. Perhaps the WWF's most
successful effort has been the .... (20) of the polar bear.

b Fill in the blanks in the following sentences by choosing a suitable form of
one word from the following lists.
- nest, habitat, reserve, den, sanctuary
- conservation, preservation, extinction, slaughter, protection, survival,
  safeguarding, exploitation

1 Who wants to go and see the zebras in the nature .... ?
2 I don't like to see animals in cages; I'd rather see them in their natural
....
3 The government should make laws to .... animals from
extinction.
4 Some pigs were being .... for their meat – there was blood
everywhere.
5 We need more .... to protect birds from being hunted.
6 The World Wildlife Fund has helped in the .... of many rare
species.
7 It has saved some of them from ....
8 The .... of the whale is now in question with all the hunting that
goes on; it may soon be extinct.
9 You should never take eggs from a bird's ....

10 'We must take measures to protect all animals from ruthless . . . . ,'
said Jolly Decent, MP for Northtown.

c Put the correct group name from the box with each group of animals.

flock	flight	herd	shoal	school	pack	troop	litter	brood

1 sheep   . . . .   7 whales   . . . .
2 birds   . . . .   8 monkeys   . . . .
3 wolves   . . . .   9 cattle   . . . .
4 dogs   . . . .   10 hens   . . . .
5 elephants   . . . .   11 goats   . . . .
6 fish   . . . .   12 puppies   . . . .

d Combine the following sentences, beginning with the words given.

1 The animals were very courageous. They defeated their human
enemies.
Thanks to . . .

2 Boxer had iron-shod hoofs. He stretched a stable-lad lifeless in the
mud.
With the help of . . .

3 We can protect wildlife by creating nature reserves.
Wildlife . . .

4 Polar bears were hunted from motorboats and aircraft. This brought
them close to extinction.
The hunting of . . .

5 Bird sanctuaries have been set up. Many nesting areas have been
protected.
Through . . .

6 The WWF provided funds. Many African countries have set up game
reserves.
Aided by . . .

7 The industrialized world has polluted the seas. Marine life has been
placed in danger.
By pollution of . . .

8 The import of certain furs was banned and this was a great step
forward.
The ban on . . .

9 People have now set up protected nesting sites for turtles. A WWF
campaign helped them to do this.
Aided by a WWF campaign . . .

10 If we destroy their natural habitat, we threaten the existence of the
animals themselves.
The destruction of . . .

4
Foul play

UNIT 13 HOOLIGANS?

1 Speaking

In pairs or groups, discuss the following questions.

1 How did sport originate? Do people take part in sport for the same reason today?

2 *'Detested sport*
That owes its pleasure to another's pain' (W Cowper)
Which sport is this true of?

3 *'... the image of war without its guilt.'* (R S Surtees)
Is this a fair description of sport?

2 Listening

Prediction

a Why do people watch sport? Discuss some of the reasons, then look at the pictures of fans below. Which words might each fan use in giving reasons?

– thrill	– attack	– frustration	– animal
– skill	– grace	– defend	– beautiful
– shout	– fitness	– wreck	

1

2

3

4

 b Now listen and find out if you are right.

Inference

 c Can you work out which sport each fan is referring to? As you listen for the second time, you may like to note down any words or phrases which provide clues.

3 Reading

Gist reading

a The following is an extract from a novel called *Fire on the Mountain* by
Anita Desai. Read it once quickly.
Do any of the characters remind you of any of the fans you heard in **2a**?

1 'Memsahib going to a party,' chanted one flop-haired
monkey, catapult in hand.
'Lace-y and tart-y,' bawled another whose weapon was a
marble as large as a horse chestnut.
5 'Silence, you bandars,' screamed Ila Das, and suddenly
opened out her umbrella and made to charge through them with
it held before her, a torn silk barricade with, she thought,
appropriately sharp spikes.
Alas, the spikes were broken. The umbrella squeaked in
10 protest. Boys fell upon it, brought it down into the dust and
it bowled along the gravel, kicked helpfully on by them to the
side of the road. If there hadn't been a fence there, it would
have gone over the edge and rolled down, down, down to the
bitter bottom of the khud – a sad balloon inflated with Ila Das's
15 dreary past. Roaring in joyous expectation, the boys tried to
help it through the rails but it stuck fast, protesting like a lady
in hoop-skirts at their uncouth sport.
Ila Das squeaked and shrilled like an agitated shrew, her little
eyes blinked tearfully behind the spectacles. 'Hooligans,' she
20 hiccuped, her voice breaking. 'I'll go straight to the Principal.
I'll report to the police . . .'

Locating specific information

b Ila Das went to the police station to make a complaint. Complete this
Police Report Form using information from the text.

Victim ....

Assailant(s) ....

Weapons ....

Injuries ....

Damage ....

Inference

c In pairs, use clues from the text to help you answer the following questions.

1 In what country does the story take place?
2 Why do the boys attack Ila Das?
3 What age are the different characters in the story?

d In pairs, discuss the following questions and answer by making a mark on the scale below. You should refer to the text for points to support your answer.

a) How does Ila Das appear in the extract?

1	2	3	4	5	6	7	8	9	10
feeble									*bold*

b) How do the boys appear?

1	2	3	4	5	6	7	8	9	10
playful									*vicious*

c) How important is the umbrella?

1	2	3	4	5	6	7	8	9	10
unimportant									*very important*

Vocabulary

e Look at these words from the text:
1 'bandar' (line 5)
2 'khud' (line 14)

They are not English words but you can work out what they mean. First, look at the words near the unknown word and decide what kind of word (verb, noun, etc.) it must be. Then, look at the events in the text and work out the approximate meaning.

f Now look at the following verbs from the text which are to do with sounds. Match the people and objects (a–f) with the verbs (1–6) and make your own sentences. How many correct sentences can you make?

Person/object	Verb
a) the referee's whistle	1 roar
b) the manager	2 scream
c) the player	3 chant
d) the turnstile	4 shrill*
e) the crowd	5 bawl
f) the fans	6 squeak

*normally an adjective only, e.g. a shrill voice

4 Grammar Participle and adjectival clauses

a Look at how we can use participle clauses to combine the sentences:

I slammed the door.   +   I left the room.

▶ a) *Slamming the door, I left the room.*
or   *Leaving the room, I slammed the door.*

I was walking to my car.   +   I felt something in my hand.

▶ b) *Walking to my car, I felt something in my hand.*

I had broken the handle.   +   I went back to apologize.

▶ c) *Having broken the handle, I went back to apologize.*

Notice that the subject of the two clauses is the same so we omit the subject in the participle clause.

Compare these two sentences:

Her uncle had left the room.   +   **I** told her my secret.

We can combine these, but because the subject of the two clauses is different we cannot omit the subject in the participle clause:

▶ d) ***Her uncle** having left the room, **I** told her my secret.*

Now combine the following pairs of sentences, using the patterns above.
1 I was going to the bus stop. I met an old friend.
2 I was running for the bus. I actually knocked into her.
3 We picked ourselves up. Then we began to chat.
4 We hadn't seen each other for ages. We had a lot to talk about.
5 I didn't notice the time. I missed my bus.
6 The bus had gone. She offered me a lift.
7 I didn't want to be late. I accepted.
8 Her son had taken the car. We were forced to travel by bus.

b Look at how a **passive** sentence can be changed into a participle clause and combined with another sentence in the same way as the active sentences we looked at in **4a**.

I was filled with anger.   +   I left the room.

▶ a) *Filled with anger, I left the room.*
or   *I left the room, filled with anger.*

I was driven out of the room.   +   I didn't know what to do next.

▶ b) *(Having been) driven out of the room, I didn't know what to do next.*

The job had been done.   +   I left the house.

▶ c) ***The job** (having been) done, I left the house.*

We can combine sentences using *be* + **adjective** (**adjectival clause**) in the same way:

I was too afraid to reply.   +   I stared at the floor.

▶ d) *Too afraid to reply, I stared at the floor.*

Now combine these pairs of sentences, using the patterns above.

1 I was asked to explain my behaviour. I made no reply.
2 I was ordered to stand for several hours. I soon grew weary.
3 My clothes had been removed. I began to shiver.
4 Their questions were unanswered. They became impatient.
5 I was amused at their failure. I laughed in their faces.
6 They were angered by my scorn. They ordered me out.
7 My clothes had been returned to me. I was free to go.
8 I was tired. I sank into a chair.
9 It was broken. It collapsed beneath me.
10 The chair leg was in my hand. I stammered an apology.

c Now look at these sentences connected with the text in **3a**. Rewrite them to make single sentences, using the patterns you practised in **4a** and **4b** above.

1 She opened out her umbrella. She charged at the boys.
2 It looked like a torn silk barricade. The umbrella was a very ineffective weapon.
3 It was broken. The umbrella squeaked in protest.
4 They had grabbed the umbrella. The boys brought it down into the dust.
5 It was kicked by the boys. It bowled along the gravel.
6 The boys were full of joy. They tried to help it through the rails.
7 Her dignity had been shattered. Ila Das squeaked shrilly.
8 She hiccuped. Ila Das called the boys 'hooligans'.
9 She screamed at them. She threatened to go to the police.
10 Their enthusiasm was spent. They had lost interest.
11 Tears were falling down her face. She screamed more loudly.
12 They had failed to kick the umbrella through the rails. The boys ran off.

5 Writing

a Describe what is happening in the pictures opposite, then put them in the order in which you think the events took place.

b Using the information in the pictures and the notes below, write a detailed
account of what happened at a recent International Table Tennis
Competition. Try to include at appropriate points in the story your own
examples of each of the structures practised in the grammar exercises in
this unit.

Examples:
- *Filled with rage, the champion swore at the umpire.*
- *Throwing his bat towards the crowd, he made angrily for the door.*
- *Furious, the woman rushed at the terrified player.*

Notes

Championship match / Players (provide names and nationalities) / Players
tense / Player A protests / Refuses to play on / Swears at umpire / Throws
bat / Hits woman / Woman screams / Crowd roars / Crowd throws
objects at players / Player A frightened / Player A hides under table /
Spectators chant / Fight breaks out / Both players hide under table /
Spectators climb on table / Table breaks / Police use tear gas / Diplomats
angry / Relations between the two countries broken off / War breaks out

UNIT 14 BE A SPORT!

1 Speaking

Discuss the following statement and the questions below.

'We can learn a lot about any society from the way it organizes its recreational activities.'

What is the most popular recreational activity in your country?

What makes it so popular?

Would you agree with the above statement?

2 Reading

Locating specific information

a You are going to read about the development of cricket, a sport popular in many countries where English is spoken.

Read the text from a magazine article and make notes to complete the table opposite.

Cricket was one of the rural recreations popular from the Middle Ages onwards among the common people. The exact historical roots and origins of the game are still the subject of considerable controversy but during the 17th century detailed records of matches began to be kept.

Such matches were played under the sponsorship of aristocrats, such as the Duke of Richmond. The matches were not only played for large sums of money but gambling was also commonplace. For example, when the Old Etonians met England in 1751 the prize was £1,500 while the side bets totalled £20,000.

It was out of a desire to strengthen their sides' capabilities that cricketing aristocrats created professional players. Patrons, such as Lord Tankerville and the Duke of Dorset, would hire the best players from the common people to come and work on their estates as gardeners and coach drivers.

As industrialization changed the geographical, social and political face of Britain, no provision was made for recreational facilities for working people. Sport was prohibited on the public roads and leisure time was severely curtailed by the enforced demands of factory life. During the second quarter of the 19th century the real low point was reached as the traditional rural forms of culture disappeared with nothing to replace them.

Cricket, therefore, developed as a sport for people to watch, rather than play. In the late 19th century the county teams began to employ professional players whose social origins and class background were quite distinct from the amateur gentleman player. These professionals were forced to use separate dressing and dining rooms, to enter the field of play through a separate gate and to refer to the amateurs as 'sir'. The professionals' reward for playing for the same county for ten years or more was a benefit match which might net them around £1,000 – a meagre £2 per week in deferred wages. And the average professional cricket player today is scarcely better off.

The development of cricket

1 Sponsored by ...? 2 Why?	
3 Who created professional players? 4 Why?	
5 The effects of industrialization ...	
6 The difference between amateur and professional players ...	

Inference

b 1 What conclusions do you draw about British society in the 18th and
19th centuries?
2 Do you think the situation is still the same today?
3 How similar is the structure of society in your own country?
4 What do you think are the political views of the writer?

Vocabulary

c Below are some useful words from the text.
1 Place each word in the appropriate column. Use a dictionary and try to
build other words from it.
2 Underline the syllable which carries the main stress. Does this change
when the grammatical function changes? Does the pronunciation of
the other syllables change?

	Noun	Verb	Adjective
1 development	development	to develop	developing
2 origin	....	....	....
3 controversy	....	....	....
4 change	....	....	....
5 provision	....	....	....
6 prohibit	....	....	....
7 curtail	....	....	....
8 reach	....	....	....
9 transform	....	....	....
10 disappear	....	....	....
11 replace	....	....	....
12 begin	....	....	....
13 improve	....	....	....
14 establish	....	....	....
15 remain	....	....	....

3 Listening

Intonation

▭ **a** Look at some of the ways we can make questions:

                                                                   Answer expected

1 Cricket began in the 17th century, didn't it?   ...
2 Cricket didn't begin in the 17th century, did it?   ...
3 Cricket began in the 17th century, didn't it?   ...
4 Cricket didn't begin in the 17th century, did it?   ...

Numbers 1 and 3, and 2 and 4 **look** the same but now listen to how they are spoken. Decide on the answer the speaker expects, and fill in the blanks with *Yes,* or *No,* or *?* if the speaker is really asking for information (a genuine 'question').
What makes the difference in meaning between 1 and 3, and between 2 and 4?

▭ **b** Listen to the following questions and mark the direction of the voice on the 'tag' (which is in italic).

Either: ↗ = A questioning tone
Or: ↘ = The speaker expects agreement

Example (question 1 in **3a** above): ↗
Cricket began in the 17th century, didn't it?

1 Cricket isn't male-dominated, *is it?*
2 Cricket's male-dominated, *isn't it?*
3 Cricket isn't male-dominated, *is it?*
4 Cricket's male-dominated, *isn't it?*

▭ **c** Listen to some more questions and mark the answer expected (*Yes, No* or *?*). Your marks should refer to the questions, not to the text you read in **2a**.

1	2	3	4	5	6	7	8	9	10

▭ **d** Listen again and this time give short answers to the questions by referring to the text in **2a**.

Confirm: *true.*
            Yes, that's ⎰ *correct.*
            No,   ⎱ *right.*

Or

Contradict: *Actually, it is/isn't.*
                In fact, it did/didn't.
                As a matter of fact, they were/weren't.

4 Listening

Note-taking

□ a Listen to the first part of a discussion about another sport. Note down which sport it is and five changes which have taken place in this sport.

Sport:

....

Changes:

1 ....

2 ....

3 ....

4 ....

5 ....

□ b Listen to the rest of the discussion. Note the main point being discussed and then the arguments for and against.

Discussion point: ....

For	**Against**
....	....
....	....
....	....
....	....

5 Grammar   Transferred negation

a Look at these sentences:

a) *I don't think tennis has changed.*
b) *I think tennis hasn't changed.*

Do the above sentences have the same meaning?
Complete this list of other verbs like *think* (verbs involving a 'mental act'),
which can be used in the same way.

1 to think   4 to s.......
2 to b.......   5 to ex.......
3 to im.......

b Using the patterns a) and b) above, and the 'mental act' verbs, make two
sentences with the same meaning for each of the following prompts. Use a
variety of verbs and tenses.
Example: She/tennis
  ▶ *I don't believe she likes tennis.*
  ▶ *I believe she doesn't like tennis.*

1 Cricket/interesting   6 The fans/disappointed
2 The home team/win   7 The stadium/full
3 The match/cancel   8 The rain/stop
4 The player/apologize   9 She/boxing
5 The crowd/enjoy the game   10 They/horse-racing

c When we add a tag to a statement, then the tag is normally the opposite of the statement:
She *likes* tennis, *doesn't* she?
She *doesn't* like tennis, *does* she?

But what is the tag for these sentences?
1 *I don't expect you brought your tennis racket, ...?*
2 *I expect you didn't bring your tennis racket, ...?*

Now add tags to the sentences you made from the prompts in **5b.** Again, make two sentences for each prompt.

d Make sentences from the prompts below, using the patterns you practised in **5c.** In pairs, respond to each other's questions.
Example: tennis/change
▶ *I don't believe tennis has changed much, has it?*
▶ *I believe tennis hasn't changed much, has it?*

1 sport/big business
2 regulations/change
3 success/most important
4 prize money/increase
5 pressure to win/decrease
6 standards of behaviour/improve
7 umpires' decisions/challenged
8 professional sportspeople/essential
9 leisure time/reduced
10 recreational facilities/wasted

6 Writing   For and against

a In examinations you may have to write essays with titles like: 'Tourism: A blessing or a curse? – Discuss'. 'International sporting events do more harm than good. – Discuss'. In this kind of essay you are expected to present your own opinions on the subject. However, you will also refer to opposing opinions before you come to a conclusion. It is important that you organize your ideas and give the essay a clear structure.

Points to remember
1 *The paragraph* – A paragraph is a unit of information and so each paragraph should deal with a separate topic.
2 *Topic sentences* – Each paragraph is usually organized around a topic sentence: this is a sentence which shows the main idea in a particular paragraph. In the following example the topic sentence begins the paragraph:

English today is a world language. It is the native language of most of the population not only of Britain but also of the USA, Canada, Australia and New Zealand. Many other countries use English as a second or additional language, for purposes including government, education, and external trade. Elsewhere, English is often taught as a foreign language.

The topic sentence is not always the first sentence:

People visit Crete for a number of very different reasons: the weather, the scenery, the archaeological sites. There is, however, one thing all visitors to Crete must not fail to visit: the Samaria Gorge. *The Samaria Gorge is one of the most remarkable sights to be found anywhere in Europe.* It is the longest gorge in Europe and it passes through landscapes of outstanding beauty. In parts, the 'walls' come very close together . . .

3 *Link words* – Within the paragraph we use certain words and phrases to connect the individual sentences and to make them 'flow'. We use words such as: *however, nevertheless, moreover, despite this fact, in addition, whereas, while, in spite of,* etc.

4 *Connecting paragraphs* – Although each paragraph is a unit of information, the paragraph in a 'for and against' essay should still show some connection with those before and after. It is also possible to start a new paragraph with one of the link words above to show a different point of view.

5 *Overall plan* – If you have to write an essay on, for example, the advantages and disadvantages of international sports competitions, you might plan your essay as follows:

Introduction
Disadvantages/arguments against
Advantages/arguments for
Conclusion

Pre-writing

b Now read the essay overleaf and try to
1 mark the points where a new paragraph begins.
2 underline all topic sentences.
3 underline all link words.
4 write what you think might have been the plan for the essay.
5 give the essay a title.

Free writing

c Using the points you have practised, plus your own ideas, write a 'for and against' discussion of the following:
'Sport brings people and players together in a spirit of healthy competition and mutual understanding.'

It is often claimed that nuclear energy is something we cannot do without. We live in a consumer society where there is an enormous demand for commercial products of all kinds. Moreover, an increase in industrial production is considered to be one solution to the problem of mass unemployment. Such an increase presupposes an abundant and cheap energy supply. Many people believe that nuclear energy provides an inexhaustible and economically realistic source of power and that it is therefore essential for an industrially developing society. There are a number of other advantages in the use of nuclear energy. Firstly, nuclear power, barring accidents, is clean. A further advantage is that a nuclear power station can be run and maintained by relatively few technical and administrative staff. The nuclear reactor represents an enormous step in our scientific evolution and, whatever the anti-nuclear lobby says, it is naïve to expect a return to more primitive sources of fuel. However, opponents of nuclear energy point out that nuclear power stations pose a direct threat not only to the environment but also to civil liberties. Furthermore, it is questionable whether ultimately nuclear power is a cheap source of energy. There have, for example, been very costly accidents in the USA, in the UK and, of course, in the Soviet Union. The possibility of increases in the cost of uranium in addition to the cost of greater safety provisions could price nuclear power out of the market. In the long run, environmentalists argue, nuclear energy wastes valuable resources and disturbs the ecology to an extent which could bring about the extinction of the human race. Thus if we wish to survive, we cannot afford nuclear energy. In spite of the case against nuclear energy outlined above, nuclear energy programmes are proliferating. Such a proliferation assumes a continual growth in industrial production and consumer demands. However, it is doubtful whether this growth will or can continue. Having weighed up the arguments on both sides, it seems there are good economic and ecological reasons for sources of energy other than nuclear power.

UNIT 15 FAIR PLAY

1 Speaking

a What does this symbol represent?
Why do you think it was chosen?

b What is the cartoonist saying in the illustration below?

2 Listening

Gist listening

a You will hear a sports commentary. Which sport is it about?

Locating specific information

b Listen again and complete the following phrases.
1 'they fought like . . . .'
2 'he . . . . the winning shot'
3 'they have been launching . . . . after attack'
4 'the team have played like . . . .'
5 'the . . . . is over'

c 1 What do the missing words in the previous exercise have in common?
2 What do they tell you about the speaker's feelings?

3 Reading

Gist reading

a   Read quickly through the following text from *Time* magazine. Is it about
   a) the 1980 Olympics?   c) the 1984 Olympics?
   b) the 1988 Olympics?   d) the 1932 Olympics?

A Glorious Ritual

Astonishing how the joy and scepticism worked together, that we could be wary of feelings of unabashed
5 celebration and clasp them nonetheless. Why in a world of real troubles should the heart leap up at the spectacle of 125 trumpeters trumpeting, 960
10 voices choiring, 1,065 high school girls (count 'em) drilling in the sun? A magic show. People turned into flags. A band became a map of the
15 United States, and the map sang "America the Beautiful". Why didn't 84 pianists in blue playing "Rhapsody in Blue" look preposterous? Why didn't
20 Rocket Man look more preposterous? We knew it would happen, yet it happened. The athletes strode in and touched us again. China
25 and Romania brought down the house. When the President said, 'I declare open the Olympic Games of Los Angeles', were we supposed to think
30 politics? When we gulped at the sight of Rafer Johnson's face, were we supposed to feel foolish?
   What were people thinking
35 in 1932, the last time clusters of Olympic athletes paraded into Los Angeles Memorial Coliseum? The world looked more perilous then; perhaps it
40 wasn't. That Depression year,

34 million Americans were out of work. One day after the 1932 Olympics began, Hitler's National Socialists won a
45 plurality of seats in the German parliament. In 1932 Mussolini told his countrymen, 'I foresee a long series of political, economic and
50 military wars.' And Aldous Huxley wrote *Brave New World*. And the opening ceremonies of the Olympic Games came off without a
55 hitch.
   Last Saturday the ritual was re-enacted, enlarged considerably from the 39 nations in 1932 to 140 this
60 year. The audience for the Games promises to be up a bit: 510,000 in 1932, more than 2 billion now. Saturday's show was brighter, brassier. Still the
65 basic ceremony held its ground. All the excitement generated by seeing the stairway ascend to the Coliseum torch was merely a
70 gloss on the fact that the torch was lighted. Everything was startling, but the same. Tunes were played. The kids marched in and out. Odd to
75 think that 52 years from now people may look back and remark with deep wisdom: How naïve they were. How mindless.
80 They would be right. A certain wilful mindlessness is

required by these events. In a way, the entire Olympics constitute a ceremony. All the
85 action is symbolic, inarticulate. What message was delivered in the Coliseum? At the ceremonies, Chief Organizer Peter Ueberroth answered
90 'world peace and under-standing', but that was merely a wishful guess. Our reaction is emotional thus mysterious. All one really knows is the
95 feeling of familiarity the ceremonies engender, the strange, abiding comfort that comes from recognizing that one has been pleased by these
100 events before, and will most likely be pleased by them again, in another time, in no particular time at all.
   Which may be the reason
105 ceremonies were invented: to hold time still by repeated practices, so that it would be difficult, or beside the point, to identify a particular date or
110 age. Blink your eyes and step out of history. Are we in London, Athens, Rome? Is that Carl Lewis or Coroebus of Elis? Time has no business in these
115 events, which makes the Olympics a kind of illusion. So be it. On Saturday, balloons filled the field like sudden blossoms, and the crowd dived
120 headlong into a recurrent dream.

Locating specific information

b   Which of the following countries is not referred to in the text? Why?
   China   United States   Germany   Italy   Russia   Greece   Romania

c Are the following statements true (T) or false (F) according to the text? Give line references to support your answers.

1 The author says 1984 was a depression year.
2 Rocket Man did not seem at all ridiculous.
3 The athletes shook hands with the spectators.
4 The audience's reaction was naive.

d Find three ways in which the Olympics of 1932 and 1984 were the same. Find three ways in which these two Games were different.

e Explain what the author means by:

1 'the map sang "America the Beautiful"' (line 15)
2 'China and Romania brought down the house' (line 24)
3 'the opening ceremonies of the Olympic Games came off without a hitch' (line 52)
4 'The audience for the Games promises to be up a bit' (line 60)
5 'the crowd dived headlong into a recurrent dream' (line 119)

Vocabulary

f Match the words from the text (1–8) with the definitions (a–h).

1 wary (line 3)   a) intentional, determined
2 unabashed (line 4)   b) repeated, occurring repeatedly
3 preposterous (line 19)   c) cautious, looking out for trouble
4 perilous (line 39)   d) difficult to put into words
5 startling (line 72)   e) ridiculous, absurd
6 wilful (line 81)   f) dangerous, full of risk
7 inarticulate (line 85)   g) very surprising
8 recurrent (line 120)   h) not embarrassed, not shy

g 1 Which of the following words from the text do **not** mean a kind of walking?

clasp leap drill stride parade blink march dive

2 Which of these words would you find in a military context?
3 Which of these words would you find in the context of sport?

h Many nouns are the roots of adjectives ending in -*less* and -*ful*. Which of the nouns below can be combined with either/both of these?

Nouns	-*less*	-*ful*	Nouns	-*less*	-*ful*
1 care	....	....	7 mind	....	....
2 end	....	....	8 will	....	....
3 harm	....	....	9 wish	....	....
4 hope	....	....	10 tune	....	....
5 use	....	....	11 play	....	....
6 worth	....	....	12 heart	....	....

Pronunciation

i Underline the main stressed syllable in the words below. What changes in stress occur as the grammatical function changes?

Noun	Verb	Adjective
celeb<u>ra</u>tion	<u>ce</u>lebrate	celeb<u>ra</u>tory
ceremony	X ·	ceremonial
familiarity	familiarize	familiar
declaration	declare	declarative
generation	generate	generative
recognition	recognize	recognizable
politics	politicize	political
economy	economize	economical
mystery	mystify	mysterious
recurrence	recur	recurrent

4 Speaking / Writing

Role-play

a The cartoon in **1b** and the reading text in **3a** touch on the political factors which lead to boycotts of the Olympic Games and at times seem to jeopardize the Games in their present form. Imagine that a special committee has been formed to consider the problems of the Games and to propose a solution. The members of the committee are:

1 A representative of the International Olympic Committee (I.O.C.)
2 A sports journalist
3 A retired athlete
4 A world-class athlete
5 A United Nations official
6 A politician
7 A representative of the Greek Olympic Committee
8 The President of the American Business Association
9 A market research expert
10 A television sports producer

Share out the roles (work in pairs or groups if necessary). Look at the following role cards or define the role in your own way.

Representative of the I.O.C.
You are conservative in your attitudes; you want things left as they are. You believe if something works, leave it alone!

A sports journalist
You feel the Games should have nothing to do with politics; that the highest standards should be aimed for both on and off the field. The Games should be exciting.

A retired athlete
In the old days the Games were not big business; athletes were patriotic and prided themselves on their physical and mental fitness. All they want now is fame and money. Give the Games to Greece!

Greek representative
The Games were born in Greece. So was democracy. Greece is the cradle of western civilization. The Games should return for good to Greece and a ceasefire be declared in all conflicts for the duration of the Games.

A politician
Your country is expecting to host the Games next time. This could mean votes for the government of which you are a member. It means profits, too. In the long-run, however, you think the USA would do the job best.

President of the American Business Association
The US finances so many sports and cultural events worldwide. The US can guarantee spectacle and commercial success. Their facilities are the best in the world. The States are a representative of the free world and the Olympic ideal.

A world-class athlete
You have a highly professional attitude. Athletes want and deserve fame and financial reward. High standards have to be paid for and athletes should be allowed to compete as individuals rather than representatives of one country.

A market research expert
Tell the meeting what the feeling is in your country at the moment according to recent surveys. (Interview people in your college/school and report back.)

A United Nations official
World peace and understanding are crucial. Politics of some nations should exclude them from the Games. You're opposed to racism in sport, and would like to see less tension between superpowers. You are sympathetic to a 'neutral' solution.

A TV sports producer
The Games are a media event; they should be spectacular and entertaining. A change in venue every four years makes for novelty; the more exotic the Games the better. It is an international event; the more nations involved the better. Use satellite potential to the full.

In your role as a member of the committee consider the following
solutions and number them 1–6 in order of preference.

1 The Olympics should always be held in Greece.
2 The Olympics should always be held in the USA.
3 The Olympics should be held in several countries at the same time.
4 The Olympics should be kept as they are now.
5 The Olympics should be abandoned completely.
6 It doesn't matter where the Olympics are held as long as athletes take
   part as individuals not as representatives of a particular country.

b Hold the meeting to present your views, take notes on the various
solutions and vote on the best one.

Summarizing

c Write a report or summary of what was said at the meeting.

Points to remember

1 Here are some of the changes we make when reporting speech:

Tenses		
Direct		**Reported**
present	→	past
present perfect	→	past perfect
past	→	past perfect
past perfect	→	past perfect
shall/will	→	should/would

Expressions of time and place		
Direct		**Reported**
today	→	*that day*
now	→	*then*
ago	→	*before*
yesterday	→	*the day before*
last week	→	*the previous week*
next year	→	*the following year*
here	→	*there*
this	→	*that*

2 For this particular topic the following will also be useful:

Suggestions/Proposals

The athlete proposed/suggested { *holding the Games in . . .*
that the Games should be held . . .

It was suggested that the Games should be held . . .
It was claimed that politics interfered with sport . . .

UNIT 16 A MARATHON RUNNER?

1 Listening

Gist listening

 1 Listen to the extract and say who is speaking and what she/he is speaking about.
2 Which words helped you guess?

2 Reading

a Read the following text (from which the key word has been omitted) and look at your answers to the previous exercise again. Were you right?

X *have embarked on a* **Marathon** *effort. To create a complete line of . . . . that can withstand the greatest tests of endurance and stamina. And now, through the efforts of* **X***'s scientists and engineers on three continents, they're here, ready to outrun every competitor in their class.*

Introducing the **X10 Series Marathon** *. . . . . , a totally new range of . . . . with an incomparable choice of features. Never before has the world seen* **Marathons** *like these. This new generation of . . . . is so advanced it can anticipate the unexpected, so intelligent it can think for itself, and so adaptable it can adjust to changing conditions.*

All in order to run and run and run. Hour after hour.

The **X10 Series Marathon** *. . . . . Built with the endurance to win.*

---

1 The missing word was:
  a) athlete/s   d) copier/s
  b) robot/s   e) coffee machine/s
  c) car/s
2 What is a 'marathon'?
  Why is this product called 'Marathon'?
3 Find words or expressions in the text which tell us that the product
  a) will work for a long time.
  b) is better than similar products.
  c) will not often need repairs.
  d) can work automatically.
  e) can do a variety of things.
  Which of these expressions could also describe an athlete?

b Now read the following more detailed advertisement for the same product and find five positive features.

A MARATHON RUNNER

Recently, **Xerox** unveiled running machines unlike any the world had ever seen. The **Xerox Marathon** copiers. The first of a new generation of copiers designed to withstand the greatest tests of endurance and stamina.

Now, the **Xerox 1035 Marathon** copier is here.

It's the world's first desktop copier that has four reduction and two enlargement modes. So you can turn an original into just about any size copy you could want. The **1035** will even select the best reduction or enlargement for your purposes, automatically. But what makes the **Xerox 1035 Marathon** outrun every competitor in its class are features you'd expect to find only in a big copier.

For instance, with the help of advanced electronic technology, the **Xerox 1035** copier is so intelligent, it can actually 'think through' difficult copy jobs and then show you how to do them. Just press the 'Help' button that's linked to a message display panel, and in plain language the **1035** can take you through what needs to be done.

Advanced electronics also enable the **Xerox 1035** to make copies so crisp and clear they're difficult to tell from the original.

And features like five contrast settings for coloured or problem originals, job interrupt and two paper trays make it hard to believe that the **1035** is only a desktop copier at a desktop copier price.

But when you see how the **Xerox 1035** is as reliable as it is advanced, you'll also see how this **Marathon** has been designed to run and run and run.

Hour after hour after hour.

The **Xerox 1035 Marathon** copier. Built with the endurance to win.

3 Grammar   Comparative clauses

a Look at the following ways of making comparisons:
   a) *X is so* + **adjective** + *(that)* **clause**
   b) *X is as* + **adjective** *as it is* + **adjective**

Examples:
   a) *The copier is so intelligent (that) it can think for itself.*
   b) *The Xerox 1035 is as reliable as it is advanced.*

XEROX, RANK XEROX, Marathon, and 1035 are trademarks.

Now use the following notes to make more comparisons.

1 advanced/anticipates the unexpected
2 adaptable/adjusts
3 complete/competitive
4 original/incomparable
5 crisp, clear/difficult to tell ...
6 intelligent/.......[Type a)]
7 well-built/.......[Type a)]
8 complete/ ....[Type b)]

b Look at these comparisons. Which is correct: *ever* or *never*?

(i) Ever/never before has the world seen Marathons *like* these.
(ii) Recently, Xerox unveiled running machines *unlike* any the world had ever/never seen.

[Note the change of position of the verb in sentence (i)]

Change these sentences to produce the alternative pattern, for example, if it is sentence type (i), change it to type (ii).

1 Never before have changes been made in cricket like those suggested today.
2 Never before have I watched a match like this one.
3 These new football boots are unlike any you have ever seen.
4 Never before has Wimbledon seen a player behave like Mac.
5 Bunter scored a goal unlike any ever recorded.
6 Mac used a tennis racket unlike any ever seen at Wimbledon.
7 Never before has the crowd watched a marathon like this one.
8 The Olympics opened with a ceremony unlike any other.

c Complete the following sentences using the patterns you practised in **3a** and **3b**. Be as imaginative as you are correct!

1 Never before have football players ...
2 Sport nowadays is so competitive ...
3 The new tennis champion is unlike ...
4 Professional sportspeople are as overpaid ...
5 Never before have hooligans ...
6 Athletes these days are so fit ...
7 The new sport of dwarf-throwing is unlike ...
8 Football managers are as self-important ...

Appreciating style

d 1 Structures like those in the exercises above are often used in advertisements. Why do you think this is so?
2 In the Xerox advertisement, why is the vocabulary borrowed from athletics?
3 Do you find this style persuasive?

4 Reading / Writing

a What would you look for if you were buying a new camera? Write down three features, then read the Canon advertisement below to see if the model has these features.

Simple yet Serious

The Canon T50 —

No film advance lever.

No complicated dials.

No exposure decisions.

Just perfect picture quality —

at a perfect price.

Canon have done it. A camera that combines the handling ease of automatic compact cameras with the picture quality of sophisticated SLRs.

The T50 has it all, starting with Auto Load. The totally automatic film advance winder means the T50 is always ready to shoot, frame after frame. And Programmed AE automatically selects the fastest shutter speed possible, giving you great action pictures and snapshots every time. What's more, the T50 can handle picture-taking in any light with the Programmed Flash AE.

Try your hand at through-the-lens creativity with the wide range of over 50 superb Canon FD lenses, including the brand-new 35–70mm, the smallest and lightest zoom lens on the market. Never before has so much been packed into a single camera body. To give handling ease plus SLR advantages at an easily affordable price. It's that simple. Seriously.

b From the following notes, and using the Xerox advertisement as a model, write an advertisement for the Canon camera.

Recently Canon unveiled a camera unlike ....
It's as simple as ....
It's so simple that ....
Never before has a camera combined ....
The T50 has been designed to .... and .... and ....
Frame after .... after ....
Never before have great action pictures ....
It's as fast as it ....
And features like the Programmed Flash AE ....
It has the best and widest range of ....
..... including the newest ....
It's the first time so much ....
The T50 is as .... as it is affordable.
It's that simple. Seriously.

Extension four

a Fill each of the numbered blanks with one suitable word.

The young champion, always the centre of .... (1) did not wait long here today to get himself into hot water again. Starting poorly, he .... (2) the first set lamely. At the start of the second set, his first three serves were called out. He .... (3) that they were in, not out, using language familiar to us all by now. Some of his fans even .... (4) the court to argue with the umpire. Fortunately, the row was .... (5) by a sudden rainstorm, as everybody ran for shelter. The break .... (6) him, and when play began again, his serve .... (7) considerably. The umpire had .... (8) any further discussion of his decisions, and the champ .... (9) to settle into his game. He .... (10) every point, but this time through skill, not gamesmanship. He .... (11) serve after serve at his opponent, who .... (12) before the onslaught. One needed no .... (13) that this was indeed the world champion; one simply .... (14) how much longer his opponent would last.

From the third set .... (15) it looked as if the fiery young player would not .... (16) up the pressure. The last set was simply .... (17), as the young champ's .... (18) enabled him to outrun his opponent. The crowd .... (19) their approval as he showed once again his determination to .... (20) the champ for another year.

b Most of the words in the list below may function as nouns or verbs without changing form, for example: *a/the coach* (noun), *to coach* (verb).

Write your own definitions for each word in the appropriate column. Include definitions for as many different meanings of the word as you can think of (the first one is done for you as an example).

1 coach	6 sponsor	11 roar	16 shoot
2 crowd	7 bat	12 net	17 score
3 match	8 patron	13 fight	18 field
4 attack	9 bet	14 fire	19 referee
5 sprint	10 chart	15 stand	20 yell

Word	Noun	Verb
1 coach	a) *person who trains athletes* b) *vehicle*	a) *teach or train*

c Fill each of the numbered gaps with one of the following words.

admit	fight	roar	hit	wonder
reached	intelligent	disappear	anticipate	provisions
effort	stamina	adaptable	replace	protest
claim	duel	scream	state	objects

The XY 98 is a car unlike any other.

Just listen to the ...... (1) of that turbo-charged engine. Makes the others sound like a ...... (2). With the XY 98 we've ...... (3) the height of engineering perfection. All the leading motor journals ...... (4) it.

Put your foot on the accelerator and watch the competition ...... (5) in the rear-view mirror. ...... (6) the brakes and feel the great machine glide to a halt. All without a word of ...... (7).

Never before has a car contained so many ...... (8) for comfort. To take the ...... (9) out of driving. And the XY 98 is designed to withstand the greatest tests of endurance and ...... (10). Built with parts you won't have to ...... (11) for thousands of kilometres.

The in-car computer is so advanced that it can ...... (12) the unexpected. So ...... (13) it can think for itself. And so ...... (14) it can adjust to changing conditions. It's not surprising the competition ...... (15). No ...... (16) we're Number 1 in the field. Other manufacturers may ...... (17) all this. We simply ...... (18) it. The XY 98 is built to triumph in any motorway ...... (19). It hardly seems a fair ...... (20).

d Rewrite the following sentences, beginning with the word(s) given, to make only one sentence.

1 I have never seen such a bad match.
   Never ...
2 It was a great match; the crowd were on their feet chanting.
   It was such ...
3 He's a good player and he's equally sporting.
   He's as ...
4 She's unlike any player I've ever seen.
   I've ...
5 He passed the ball to Robertson and ran towards the penalty area.
   Passing ...
6 McEnroe would not take part in the tournament. He had broken his leg.
   Having broken ...
7 She was furious with the umpire, and so she started to swear.
   Furious ...
8 Man of the match was Robert Taylor. He had a tremendous game.
   Robert Taylor ...
9 Gamble cut down Tanner in the eighth minute.
   It was ...
10 Detailed records were not kept until the 17th century.
   It was ...

5
It takes two

1 Speaking   Look at the illustration. What view does it present of the relationship between the sexes. Would you agree/disagree?

2 Listening

Inference

 a   You will hear part of a scene from a novel. First listen to extract 1 and answer the following questions.

1 What is the relationship between the speakers?
2 Where do you think they are?

▭ **b** Now listen to extracts 1 and 2 and answer these questions.

1 Are they married people?
2 Is there any similarity with the illustration?
3 Why does she say, 'You take mine and I'll take yours'?

Prediction

▭ **c** Listen to extract 3 and each time the tape stops, predict what the speaker might say next.

Inference

▭ **d** Now listen to all three extracts. Score a point each time either speaker makes a remark which 'puts the other person down', that is, tries to silence the other person with a criticism or hurtful comment, e.g. 'My dear woman, if I had wanted to put my hands on you, I would have done it.'

The battle of the sexes	
Woman	**Man**

e What kind of novel do you think these extracts come from? When do you think it was written?

Intonation

▭ **f** Listen to extract 3 again. Each time the tape stops try to summarize the speaker's mood with one of the following words. One has been done for you.

triumphant	cool	pitying	uninterested	doubtful
superior	angry	amused	vengeful	
confident	sweet	surprised	aggressive	

Example:
1 *angry* 4 .... 7 .... 10 .... 13 ....
2 .... 5 .... 8 .... 11 ....
3 .... 6 .... 9 .... 12 ....

Prediction

g In male/female pairs, discuss what you think will happen to the speakers next.

3 Reading

a Now read the next part of the novel *Soldier's Pay* by William Faulkner and see if you were right.

She looked at him across her shoulder from beyond an inaccessible barrier. His anger grew. 'Don't ruin my clothes, please,' she said icily. 'Here, if you must.' She raised her face and Jones felt the shame, but his boyish vanity would not let him stop now. Her face a prettiness of shallow characterless planes blurred into his, her mouth was motionless and impersonal, unresisting and cool. Her face from a blur became again a prettiness of characterless shallowness, icy and remote, and Jones, ashamed of himself and angry with her therefore, said with heavy irony: 'Thanks'.

'Not at all. If you got any pleasure from it you are quite welcome. Let me pass please.'

He stood awkwardly aside. Her frigid polite indifference was unbearable. What a fool he had been! He had ruined everything.

'Miss Saunders,' he blurted. 'I – forgive me: I don't usually act that way, I swear I don't.'

She spoke over her shoulder. 'You don't have to, I suppose? I imagine you are usually quite successful with us?'

b Who won the battle this time? Find phrases from the text to support your judgement and discuss your reasons with your partner.

Vocabulary

c 1 Make a list of the nouns, adjectives and adverbs used to describe each of the two characters.

Her	Him
inaccessible	*anger*
icily	*boyish*

2 How many prefixes and suffixes are there in your lists? What do you notice about the prefixes and suffixes in the '**Her**' column?

d Look at the nouns in the table below. Make as many adjectives as you can by adding or removing a suffix or by making any other changes necessary. You can use the same suffix more than once.

Noun	Suffix	Adjective
1 coolness	*-ful*	*cool*
2 shame	*-less*	*shameful, shameless*
3 irony	*-y*	. . . .
4 uninterest	*-ish*	. . . .
5 courtesy	*-ic*	. . . .
6 politeness	*-ive*	. . . .
7 anger	*-ing*	. . . .
8 vanity	*-ous*	. . . .
9 prettiness	*-able*	. . . .
10 pity	*-ed*	. . . .
11 boy	*-ness*	. . . .
12 ice	*-ity*	. . . .
13 doubt		. . . .
14 aggression		. . . .
15 awkwardness		. . . .
16 revenge		. . . .
17 superiority		. . . .
18 remoteness		. . . .

4 Writing

a Notice how we can describe mood in direct speech:

'Thanks,' he said $\Big\{$ *with irony* (**with** + **noun**)
ironically (**adverb**)

Complete the following including both the above patterns and using vocabulary from **3d**.

Discuss and compare your answers.

After a while, hearing no further sound of movement, Jones looked up. She stood relaxed against the table.

'Well, this was obviously not one of my successes,' he said . . . . (1).

'Hardly,' she said . . . . (2).

'I suppose I'd better go,' he said . . . . (3).

'Just when the conversation was becoming interesting?' she asked
. . . . (4).

'My conversation is always interesting,' he replied . . . . (5),
moving towards the door.

'I must say, I wasn't bored,' she admitted . . . . (6), as she
suddenly flung herself into an armchair.

He turned. 'No. You must have found the whole thing quite amusing,' he said . . . . (7).

b Now continue this episode yourself. Include both action and dialogue and
base it on the following 'scenario':

She is at first aggressive; makes him feel humiliated. The experience
amused and embarrassed her; she likes men who amuse her; one thing he
can't cope with is indifference; she offers him a drink; he refuses and
makes for the door; she wonders whether he always retreats when the
battle is difficult; he claims he has other battles to fight; she finds cowards
irresistible . . .

In *Soldier's Pay* the episode ends with the following:

> . . . and Jones did not know the door had opened until she jerked
> her mouth from his and twisted slimly from his grasp.

UNIT 18 MAKING PEACE

1 Speaking

Do you agree with any of the following statements? Discuss in groups.

1 The husband should be responsible for supporting the family.
2 Everything in the house should belong to the man.
3 Parents must provide a dowry for their daughter.
4 Women should have no legal rights over children.
5 The children's education should be the mother's responsibility.
6 If a husband goes to prison, he loses his rights over the children.

2 Reading / Speaking

Note-taking

a The following text refers to marriage legislation in a particular European country. Make notes about what the law says about the statements in 1 above.

- The man must support the family, i.e. wife and children. *If* the wife has property then she must share this responsibility according to her income or property.

5 - Property previously owned by the wife remains hers unless she signs it over to another. However the woman may make claim for property acquired during the marriage as a result of them both working. Furnishings: everything that is in the household belongs to the man unless the woman can prove by receipts that she bought 10 it. Her personal effects belong to her. She has the right to the things she needs absolutely, e.g. a sewing machine, unless the man claims them too.

- Dowry – a separate and parallel system.
When parents have property they are obliged to give a dowry to their daughter of value in proportion to their personal 15 property, the number of children, and the social rank of the bridegroom. This dowry usually remains the property of the woman, but the husband has the administration and the income of the dowry. Although the concept and practice of dowry is changing, technically a daughter may sue her parents 20 for a dowry if and when they can afford it.

- Children

Paternal Authority: The male is the head of the household, and apart from nursing, women have no legal rights over their children. The father has the right to decide everything for the 25 children, e.g. he is obliged to educate them, and the children cannot leave the country without his official permission. Parental rights (i.e. upbringing, supervision, education, residence and disciplinary measures) and representation of the

child are carried by the father, e.g. administration of the child's property.
30 *Should* the father abuse these rights, or if he is dead, missing or 'incapable',
the mother automatically becomes guardian of her children. In cases where
the mother wants to remarry, she must apply to the court in order to remain
guardian. *When* there is no mother, of *if* she is declared 'incapable', a third
person (e.g. grandfather) is appointed guardian. The father forfeits paternal
35 authority *if* he is condemned to imprisonment for at least one month for an
unlawful act against the life, health or morality of the child. Paternal authority
ends *if* the father or the child dies or disappears, or through the child's
becoming adult. *In the event of* bankruptcy, the father is deprived of the
administration of the child's property, and the court will appoint a guardian.

Vocabulary

b 1 Complete the following with the appropriate adjective for each noun.

father: *paternal*   mother: ....
parent: ....   marriage: ....
brother: ....   matrimony: ....

2 Underline the formal (F) words in the following list, then match them
with their informal (I) synonyms.
Example: *effects* (F) = *things* (I)

have to	residence	forfeit	position
concept	acquire	do away with	permission
supervise	look after	deprive	things
idea	get	be obliged to	home
effects	take away from	consent	
rank	abolish	lose	

Discussion

c Discuss what you know about family law in your own or any other
country. How does it differ from what you have just read?

3 Listening

Locating specific information

a You will hear a Minister for Justice being interviewed about a bill for a
new family law. Listen and note three differences between the proposed
law and the previous law (which you read about in **2a**).

Prediction

b What is the last thing said by the Minister? How do you think she might
have continued?

4 Grammar   Conditional sentences

a   The conjunctions (1–5) below can all be used to introduce a condition. Complete each sentence so that it means the same as the example.
Example:
If the parents don't provide a dowry, the daughter can sue them.
1 When the parents ...
2 In cases where the parents ...
3 Should the parents ...
4 In the event of the parents ...
5 Unless the parents ... (Be careful here!)

b   The following conjunctions can also introduce a condition:
provided (that)   on condition that   so long as
as long as   providing (that)

Compare the sentences below. In which sentence does the conjunction mean 'if and only if'?
1 If the wife wants to remarry, she must apply to the court to remain guardian.
2 Provided (that) the court agrees, she can remain guardian.
Try using each of the conjunctions above to replace those in sentences 1 and 2. Does the meaning change?

c   Complete the following sentences to show the conditions you might make for a marriage. Use as many different ways of introducing the conditions as possible. (You can favour the husband or wife, as you like.)
Example:
When either partner leaves the top off the toothpaste, he/she will have to pay a fine.

1 ... , he/she will have to pay a fine.
2 He/she should be given three weeks paid holiday every year ...
3 He/she will have equal responsibility for the cooking ...
4 ... , the in-laws* will not be allowed to stay more than two hours.
5 ... , the in-laws will be allowed to stay for the whole weekend.
6 If he/she refuse to clean the house, ...
7 ... , he/she will have to remain silent for a whole week.
8 ... , he/she will not be allowed to drive the family car.
9 ... , he/she will take charge of the family's finances.
10 ... , he/she will not have to go out to work.
11 ... , he/she will not be allowed to speak to members of the opposite sex.
12 Should the marriage fail, ...

Can you think of any other conditions for a marriage?

* relatives by marriage

5 Writing

Appreciating style

a Look at each of the following statements and decide whether it is formal (F), informal (I) or neutral (N).

1 Both spouses shall have equal responsibility for the education of the children.
2 The wife needn't have a dowry.
3 The husband is under no obligation to assist in household tasks.
4 All household duties shall remain the sole responsibility of the wife.
5 The wife should be able to go out to work if she wants to.
6 Both husband and wife should have their own bank account.
7 If the couple get a divorce, the children should live with their mother.
8 Should the couple agree on their incompatibility, divorce proceedings may be initiated.
9 The wife will have to get her husband's written permission if she wants to buy anything worth more than £1,000.
10 Both spouses will be at liberty to contract extra-marital relationships if they so desire.

Pre-writing

b Using what you know about the present law in your own country or your own ideas, rewrite the text in **2a**. Keep the language **formal**.
The following headings may be useful:

1 Financial support   5 Children's upbringing
2 Ownership of property   6 Children's education
3 Dowry   7 Children's property
4 Divorce and alimony

Free writing

c Imagine that you are subject to the law outlined in **2a**. Write a letter to a magazine explaining the changes you would like to see made. Keep your language **informal** or **neutral**.

UNIT 19 A COMIC AFFAIR?

1 Speaking

The two pictures below are from the beginning of a romance comic strip story. Look at the pictures and discuss your answers to the questions.

Picture 1

1 Why is the man standing, arms in the air?
2 Why is the woman not standing?
3 What has happened to their car?
4 What is the person who is driving thinking?

Picture 2

1 Is Diana badly hurt?
2 How does the man with her feel?
3 What is the relationship between Diana and the two men?
4 What will happen next?

2 Reading / Speaking

a The pictures (1–5) opposite are in the correct order. Check whether you were right about what happens next. Then match the following captions and dialogues a)–j) with the correct picture. The first caption is done for you.

a) Don't worry, Diana, it's not far now.
b) They lived on the other side of town so I had plenty of time to think things over.
c) OK, Chuck.
d) Chuck, I'm so grateful for your help.
e) I picked her up as gently as I could. ①
f) Diana was still semi-conscious when we finally got to the hospital. I thought she was too stunned to speak, and then . . .
g) I'm taking her straight to the hospital. I'll send a pick-up truck for your car.
h) I only hope there is nothing wrong with her – she's such a delicate creature.
i) I could hardly believe that it was Diana beside me. And none of the other guys around.
j) Gee, it was nothing, and I'm staying right here until your folks arrive.

b Discuss the following questions.
  1 What more have you learnt about the relationship between Chuck and Diana?
  2 From whose viewpoint is the story told?
  3 How do you think the story will continue?

3 Grammar Special uses of comparatives

a   Diana and Chuck have known each other since they were children.
As Diana became more beautiful, so Chuck's love for her grew.
As Chuck got older, so he thought more about her.
We can say these sentences in another way:

The more beautiful Diana became, the more his love for her grew.
The older Chuck got, the more he thought about her.

Now change the following sentences in the same way. (Be careful of the word order.)
1   As Diana got older, so she became more beautiful.
2   As she became more beautiful, so her popularity increased.
3   As her circle of friends grew wider, so Chuck saw less of her.
4   As the years went by, so he grew more disheartened.
5   As he grew disheartened, so he tried to forget her.
6   As he tried to forget her, so the pain increased.
7   As the pain increased, so he became more withdrawn.
8   As he became more withdrawn, so he had less chance of attracting her.

b   Chuck did not want to show his feelings and therefore he avoided Diana.
We can say this in a different way:

Rather
Sooner   } *than show his feelings, he avoided her.*

Basing your answers on the comic strip story make similar sentences from the following.
1   Chuck did not want to wait for an ambulance.
2   Andy did not want to leave his car on the road.
3   Chuck did not want to take any risks on the way to hospital.
4   Chuck did not want to disturb Diana.
5   He did not want to leave Diana alone in the hospital.
6   He did not want to read while waiting.
7   He did not want to talk to anyone.
8   He did not want to tell Diana how he felt.

c   Now talk about Diana by completing the following. Base it on the story so far but use your imagination.
1   The older she grew, ...
2   The more friends she had, ...
3   Sooner than stay at school, ...
4   The less she saw of Chuck, ...
5   Rather than get married young, ...

4 Listening

Prediction

a Diana is in hospital and Chuck visits her on four occasions. Look at the pictures below, particularly the facial expressions. Put the numbers 1–8 in the boxes to show the correct order. The first one is done for you.

b Listen to the tape and see if you were right.

Inference

 c Listen again and decide whether the following are true (T) or false (F), by listening carefully to the speaker's tone of voice. Put (?) for 'don't know'.
a) Diana was annoyed that Chuck had waited.
b) Chuck was pleased that he had waited.
c) Chuck was pleased that Diana had a lot of visitors.
d) Chuck was surprised to find Diana alone one day.
e) Diana was disappointed with her friends.
f) Diana was glad Chuck had brought some music.
g) Diana was bored with Chuck visiting her every day.

Vocabulary

d How many correct idioms from the pattern **verb + noun + preposition** can you make from the following?

Verb	Noun	Preposition
make	fun	of
take	touch	with
catch	sight	
lose	advantage	
	a fuss	
	care	
	use	

Choose one of the idioms you have formed to complete each of the following sentences.
1 Andy had crashed, because he ...
2 As Chuck's car turned the corner, he ...
3 When Chuck was a shy little boy, people ...
4 Now that Diana is in hospital, Chuck ...
5 Chuck had always wanted ...
6 Diana's friends visited her often at first, but later they ...
7 Chuck was able to see her every day and he ...
8 Diana became very fond of Chuck because he ...

5 Speaking

a Look at the picture opposite. Chuck and Diana seemed so happy together, but now ...

In groups, discuss what you think has happened. The teacher will give one student in each group the explanation. The others must find out by asking that student questions, but only questions which can be answered by 'Yes' or 'No'.

b Who do you think this story was written for? Compare your answers. Discuss whether you think it was successful and give your reasons.

6 Writing

Look back to the beginning of the unit and rewrite the story from Diana's point of view.
Example:
Picture 1 page 98

I felt really awful; how embarrassing! I must have broken a leg or something. Then I saw a car coming.

Picture 2

A few moments later I heard someone asking me about the accident; it sounded like Chuck; I hadn't seen him for ages . . .

Complete the story in any way you like. Give it a happy ending or a miserable ending – it's up to you.

1 Speaking

a Look at the pictures below and in pairs or groups discuss your answers to the following questions.

1 What feelings do the pictures arouse in you? Would you use any of the following words to describe your feelings?

embarrassing	unusual	normal	idealistic
effeminate	abnormal	silly	common
masculine	unnatural	natural	vulgar

2 Do you consider the situations illustrated to be common today?

b Think of your ideal man or woman. How many of the following words would you use in describing them? Compare and discuss your results with other members of the class.

Nouns	Man	Woman
protection	....	....
defence	....	....
attack	....	....
pity	....	....
authority	....	....
discipline	....	....
karate	....	....
ambition	....	....
power	....	....
guardian	....	....

Adjectives	Man	Woman
physical	....	....
logical	....	....
intellectual	....	....
superior	....	....
courteous	....	....
vengeful	....	....
sweet	....	....
aggressive	....	....
sensitive	....	....
vain	....	....

2 Listening

You will hear part of a radio programme. Look at the following statements and discuss what you think you are going to hear. Then listen and choose the best answer a), b), c) or d).

1 a) There are fewer attacks on women now.
 b) There has been a violent incident recently.
 c) Violence amongst women has increased.
 d) Violence against women has increased.

2 Anna decided to learn karate because she
 a) felt tired lifting heavy boxes.
 b) felt afraid to go to bed at night.
 c) wanted to learn how to fight.
 d) had had enough of being thought weak.

3 Since she learnt karate, Mary
 a) has stopped hiding.
 b) has lost weight.
 c) feels less awkward.
 d) feels taller.

4 Anna advises women who think they are going to be attacked to
 a) try and escape.
 b) fight fire with fire.
 c) scream as loud as they can.
 d) start whistling.

5 If a woman is attacked from behind, she should try to
 a) punch her attacker.
 b) kneel down.
 c) throw the man off.
 d) grab the man's arms.

3 Reading

a Read the text below and in groups, discuss your answers to the following questions.
1 Who do you think wrote the text?
2 Who is it written for?

Practical hints

We think that karate is the ideal form of self-defence for mind and body. But it takes time to learn the techniques and absorb the attitude, so meanwhile here are some instant hints for defending yourself. Obviously violence shouldn't be used indiscriminately. It isn't always the solution any more than is compliance, but it's important to have every option at your fingertips.

If you think someone is about to attack you, start running suddenly and shout (don't scream, which is the expected response). Break a window or something that makes a lot of noise to attract attention. Carry a whistle or a small siren which you can use to make a lot of noise.

If you are grabbed and held from behind, concentrate on kicking him. Kick low and hard from the knee, aim at his shins and kneecaps; kneecaps are sensitive and can be dislodged by hard kicks. And stamp hard on his instep. Better still – though this requires practice – bend your knees, lowering yourself until your bottom is at least as low as his groin, then bend right forward and jerk your hips to one side, flinging him off.

If he's got his arm around your neck, choking you, turn your head into the crook of his elbow so that you can breathe. Kick his shins, stamp on his instep and bring your elbows back hard into his ribs.

If he is strangling you from behind with his hands, grab his little fingers and pull them back hard; at the same time scrape your heel down his shin on to his instep.

If he is facing you and trying to hit you, turn sideways so there's less of you he can hit.

If he grabs you from the front, bring your fist up under his chin or nose – hitting his nose will at least make his eyes water and force him to loosen his hold on you.

---

b 1 Think back to what you heard in **2.** Which points in the text above were also referred to by Anna and Mary? Underline them.
2 Did Anna or Mary leave out any useful information when they were giving advice? If so, what?

Vocabulary

c Write the appropriate number from the diagram next to each word in this list.

heel ☐	wrist ☐	ribs ☐	
armpit ☐	calf ☐	instep ☐	
upper arm ☐	kneecap ☐	ankle ☐	
biceps ☐	bottom ☐	sole ☐	
crook of the arm ☐	shin ☐	thigh ☐	
elbow ☐	groin ☐	fist ☐	
forearm ☐	hip ☐		

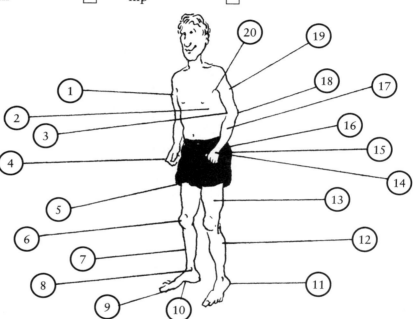

4 Grammar *it*-type and *what*-type cleft sentences

a Suppose, when talking about self-defence, someone says:

You should kick your attacker's **bottom**.

If you don't agree you can correct this in speech by stressing the new or contrasting information:

                  1   2

No, | you should kick | his *shins*.

In writing, you can do it like this. Fill in the boxes.

           2   1

It is [＿＿＿＿] (that) [＿＿＿＿＿＿]

b Look at these two sentences:

It's his shins you should kick.
It's Mary who/that kicked his shins.

Why do we have to use *who/that* in the second sentence above?

Change the following sentences to stress the new information given in brackets.
Example:
Mary felt petrified during the day.   (the night)
▶ *It was during the night (that) Mary felt petrified.*

1 Mary was terrified in the street.	(at home)
2 Anna was the first to take up karate.	(Mary)
3 Mary started karate for some exercise.	(for self-protection)
4 Mary now accepts her weight.	(height)
5 Mary had always been seen as someone frail.	(Anna)
6 Anna finally fought back in Vienna.	(Paris)
7 Anna dropped a packet of Gauloises.	(her attacker)
8 Anna took up karate to help her to fight.	(get work)

c According to the interview, this statement is also false:

1	2	3
You need	a lot of strength	to learn karate.

Correct the statement and stress the new information, completing the boxes below:

1		2	3
What	*is*	. . . .	. . . .

Now put the words in the following sentences in the correct order to make a sentence as in the pattern above.

1 you / a / carry / what / is / whistle / should
2 is / off / what / ought to / him / you / do / fling
3 his / aim at / must / what / kneecaps / you / are
4 grab / you / are / what / should / little fingers / his
5 not / what / scream / must / you / is / do
6 try / what / is / to hit / should / his / you / nose
7 is / indiscriminate violence / ought not / what / to do / you / use
8 important / every option / to have / is / what / is / your fingertips / at

d According to the interview, the following statements are false. Listen to it again and note the correct information in each case. Then correct the statements using the patterns in **4b** or **4c**.

1 There has been an increase in violence amongst women.
2 Men are supposed to be weak.
3 Anna was terrified of someone breaking into the flat.
4 Mary took up boxing for self-protection.

5 'Women's Half Hour' affected Mary's attitude towards her body.
6 Mary used to avoid wearing trousers.
7 Anna went to Budapest with her sister a couple of weeks ago.
8 The man won the brawl in Paris.
9 You must always scream when attacked.
10 It's a good idea to carry a knife.

5 Writing

Write a summary of the reading text using the verbs below.

1 If you think someone is about to attack you ...
   run/shout/scream/break/carry
2 If you are grabbed and held from behind, ...
   kick/stamp/bend/jerk/fling
3 If he's got his arm around your neck, choking you, ...
   turn/kick/stamp/bring
4 If he is strangling you from behind with his hands, ...
   grab/pull/scrape
5 If he is facing you and trying to hit you, ...
   turn
6 If he grabs you from the front, ...
   bring/hit/force/loosen

Extension five

a Fill each of the numbered blanks with one suitable word.

Women who have learnt karate no longer feel vulnerable, so if they are hassled in the street they are less frightened. We asked Anna what she would . . . . (1) if she was attacked.

'Well, it . . . . (2) depend on the circumstances. I have . . . . (3) myself against some men. I was walking with a friend in Shaftesbury Avenue when . . . . (4) blokes blocked our path and tried . . . . (5) pick us up. I took up . . . . (6) fighting stance and said "You're in . . . . (7) way". They backed away. But sexual . . . . (8) is sometimes just a ritual and it . . . . (9) me very uncomfortable about reacting aggressively.'

. . . . (10) real problem is deciding whether the situation calls for self-defence . . . . (11) for a quick escape out of danger. . . . . (12) we talked to the women, we began . . . . (13) see that gaining physical strength was radically . . . . (14) how they felt about themselves, and greatly . . . . (15) their self-confidence. We slowly understood that . . . . (16) breaks down the division between mind . . . . (17) body. We also asked the women if . . . . (18) were worried about experiencing anger and aggression. They said that karate makes you . . . . (19) confident you can deal with a . . . . (20) situation without becoming aggressive.

b Fill each of the blanks in the following sentences with a suitable word or phrase.

1 A man . . . . out at Mary from a dark corner as she was on her way home.
2 She . . . . up a fighting stance and he ran away frightened.
3 She ran after him but he . . . . away.
4 We musn't . . . . sight of the main purpose of karate, which is self-defence.
5 If a man attacks you from behind you should try and . . . . him off.
6 Women who live alone often feel . . . . to attack.
7 He's a . . . . friend – you can be sure he'll stand by you when you're in trouble.
8 He's so generous that people take . . . . of him.
9 Some men refuse to do the housework because they're afraid people will . . . . of them.
10 I caught . . . . of him as he was leaving the building but I didn't speak to him.

c 1 Decide whether the following are parts of the leg or arm. Place them under the correct heading, in correct order from the top of the leg or arm downwards.

heel	crook	fist	wrist
armpit	sole	shin	forearm
biceps	elbow	ankle	thigh
kneecap	calf	instep	

Leg	Arm

2 Match the following, as in the example:

paternal   marriage
parental   mother
marital   father
matrimonial   brother
fraternal   parent
maternal   matrimony

3 Give the adjective form of the following nouns.

Noun	Adjective
1 anger	. . . .
2 shame	. . . .
3 vanity	. . . .
4 irony	. . . .
5 courtesy	. . . .
6 revenge	. . . .
7 superiority	. . . .
8 remoteness	. . . .
9 aggression	. . . .
10 doubt	. . . .

d Re-order the following jumbled words and phrases to make correct sentences.

1 had / Andy / loved / Diana / always
2 Chuck / loved / had / always / Diana / was / it / Andy / who / not
3 crashed / his / Chuck / with / Diana / car / driving / while
4 Chuck / was / Andy / who / car / crashed / his / it / not
5 broken / Diana / arm / her / had
6 leg / arm / broken / Diana / her / had / was / it / that / not / her
7 school / at / were / they / when / Chuck / with / Diana / love / in / fell
8 beautiful / more / as / became / Diana / older / got / so / she
9 avoided / her / sooner / feelings / Chuck / than / his / show / Diana
10 felt / rather / he / Diana / avoided / than / tell / how / her / he

6
Bright sparks

1 Speaking

a   Look at these pictures of six famous people. How many do you know? Match the names to the pictures.

a) Jane Austen   d) William Shakespeare
b) Mohandas Gandhi   e) Marie Curie
c) Wolfgang Amadeus Mozart   f) Albert Einstein

b   Which of the above would you consider to be a genius and why?

c Discuss the following statements about creativity with your partner.

	Text E	Text F
1 There is no connection between intelligence and creativity.		
2 Some form of training assists creativity.		
3 Every one of us can be considered creative.		
4 Intelligence tests do not measure creativity.		
5 Personality factors are an important part of creativity.		
6 The sign of genius is consistent creativity.		

Use the following expressions:

$$I \left\{ \begin{matrix} \textit{partly} \\ \textit{largely} \\ \textit{completely} \end{matrix} \right\} \begin{matrix} \textit{agree.} \\ \textit{disagree.} \end{matrix} \qquad I \left\{ \begin{matrix} \textit{agree} \\ \textit{disagree} \end{matrix} \right\} \left\{ \begin{matrix} \textit{to a certain} \\ \textit{to some} \end{matrix} \right\} \textit{extent.}$$

2 Reading

Jigsaw reading

a In pairs, one of you read text **E** on page 199 and the other read text **F** on page 200. Note the places where the writer makes a comment on one of the statements in **1c**. Then compare your information with your partner and together complete the table.

Vocabulary

b 1 Look at the following expressions from the texts and work out their meaning.

a) Even if a genius was needed to take the step, *the time was ripe* for it to be taken.　(text **F**, line 25)

b) But if there is such a factor, *we have no inkling* as to what it might be.　(text **F**, line 67)

c) It is probably only *a layman's idea* that . . .　(text **E**, line 1)

d) Many regard this as unfortunate, but *the custom seems to have prevailed*.　(text **E**, line 37)

e) Terman's study . . . does not *throw much light on* this theory.　(text **E**, line 61)

2 Do the following expressions in italics have a similar meaning to each other?

a) Creativity *is bound up with* intelligence.

b) There is *a connection between* creativity *and* intelligence.

c) There is evidence of substantial *correlations between* IQ *and* certain creative talents.

3 The word *distinguish* is used several times in the texts. How many examples can you find? Is the meaning always the same?

4 The following expressions can be used to talk about the same thing. What might it be?

a) positive correlation　b) criteria　c) to validate

3 Grammar Concessive clauses

a Look at this sentence from text **F**:
However gifted, the outstanding man still needs training.
Do the following clauses have a similar meaning to *However gifted*?
1 Although he is gifted . . .
2 It doesn't matter how gifted he is . . .
3 Because he is gifted . . .
4 No matter how gifted he is . . .

b You can make other words like *however* (meaning 'It doesn't matter' or 'No matter . . . .') by taking *Wh*-question words and adding **-ever**, for example: *whatever*. Think of four more examples.

c Look at these two sentences and say which is correct according to the texts. Why is the other wrong?
a) However small, we are all capable of creative acts.
b) We are all capable of creative acts, however small.

Ignoring the blanks, look at the following sentences and decide whether you need to change the order of the clauses in any of them.
Then complete the sentences using one of the words you formed in **3b**.
1 . . . . the scientist, it was a remarkable discovery.
2 . . . . the problem, a solution can often be found.
3 . . . . impractical it may be, intelligence tests should include a measure of creativity.
4 . . . . interesting, the study did not throw much light on the theory.
5 . . . . possible, such tests should be validated.
6 . . . . is chosen, you can find defects in any test.
7 . . . . the writer, he seems to agree with the research.
8 . . . . talented, education can still benefit the genius.
9 . . . . available, the full account of the original experiment should be consulted.
10 . . . . he is born, the genius benefits many countries.

d Look at these three examples of **concessive clauses:**
a) *Whatever he plays, he does it brilliantly.*
b) *No matter how gifted (he is), he still needs to practise.*
c) *It doesn't matter who his audience is, he's always nervous before a performance.*

Now make a similar sentence for each of the following.
1 He's clever, but he still makes mistakes.
2 Education may be useful, but it cannot create geniuses.
3 Examine any century and you can find outstanding thinkers.
4 You may have a high IQ but you are not necessarily a genius.
5 I don't care who the writer is, he doesn't know what he is talking about.
6 There is always a counter-argument to any theory.

e Now add clauses to produce similar sentences from the ideas below.
1 I still find English difficult.
2 I will never/always enjoy studying.
3 I will always/never have enough money.

4 Writing

Pre-writing

a The following is a summary of text **F** in on page 200. Fill in the blanks with an appropriate link word or phrase.

We are unable to explain the nature of creative talent because we know too little about human personality to account for the different levels of achievement in creative performance. One view, ... (1), is that the difference is one of degree, not one of kind.

The first evidence for . . . . . . (2) is when two people come up with the same discovery or invention at the same time, ... (3) the calculus or the Darwinian theory of evolution. It is clear that both the individual's genius and the accompanying circumstances contributed in these cases.

It is . . . . (4) clear that a gifted person needs training and practice as well as outside help and stimulation. Many famous theories were the result of their originators reading other people's work. By responding to similar influences we can all be creative at times.

The great artist and thinker is different in being consistent in his output, probably because he is better in some way or ways. There may . . . . (5) be some factor which distinguishes the outstanding from the average person, ... (6) what that factor is is unknown.

When we are able to understand 'personality', we may . . . . (7) understand creative thinking. The same factors account for the extent and the nature of individual ability.

Summarizing

b Write about 200 words summarizing text **E** on page 199.

Points to remember
- Make notes of the main points in each paragraph.
- Fill in any missing steps in the argument.
- Go back to the original text and check that nothing essential has been missed out.

Your answers to the following questions should help you with the main points of text **E**.
1 How is the creative person different from the rest of us?
2 With what is creativity usually linked?
3 Do studies prove conclusively that children with high IQs are likely to develop into geniuses?
4 What makes it difficult to prove there is a correlation?
5 What do intelligence tests measure and what do they leave out?

5 Speaking

a Text E talked about an age level 'recognized as the most creative' –
childhood. Look at these examples of children solving the problem of
how to stop a cat and dog fighting.

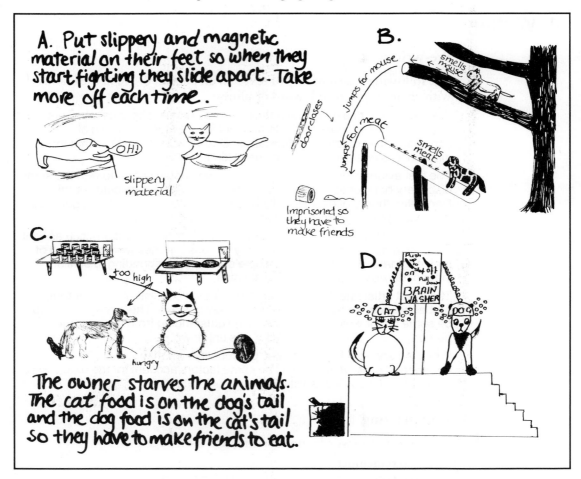

b 1 Describe how each solution works.
2 Match each with one of these concepts:
   • the gradual approach
   • direct-love
   • mutual-aid
   • 'let them get on with it'
3 Place the solutions in order, according to how effective each would be.
   Say why they would or would not be effective.
4 Then place them according to imagination and originality, and give
   your reasons.
   Is the order the same as in 3?

c Now it's your turn. Can you solve the following problem?

> Five men are seated around a table. None of them has a left arm. A servant brings in a paper parcel. This is unwrapped to reveal a severed left arm. After everyone has inspected the arm, they smile, apparently with satisfaction, and leave the room.

Explain?
Do you think this is a useful test of any sort?

d In groups, discuss the following questions.
1 It has been estimated that only about two in a million people become really distinguished. Why do you think this is so?
2 Why do so many geniuses come from families who are far from distinguished?
3 With today's modern education why do we not produce more geniuses?

1 Speaking

Look at the diagram of the human brain and answer the following questions.
1 What information does the diagram give us?
2 What is the brain responsible for? What does it control?
3 How do you think scientists discovered these facts about the brain?
4 Is this sort of knowledge useful? In what way?

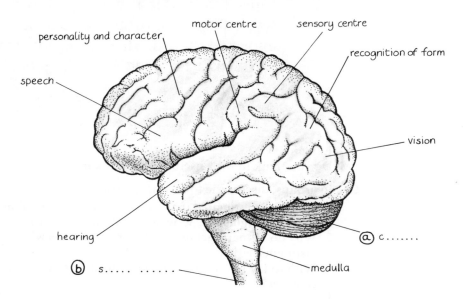

2 Listening

Gist listening

a You are going to hear a short talk about the human brain. Find out what the Ancient Greeks knew about the brain.

Locating specific information

b Listen again and complete the blanks in the following text.

Studies of the human brain have revealed some . . . . (1) of how this important organ might have . . . . (2) over millions of years. The Ancient Greeks were aware that the human brain was divided into several separate . . . . (3), or brains, each of which apparently had specific . . . . (4). In the area where the spinal cord enters the brain, for example, the cord . . . . (5) into a structure sometimes . . . . (6) by the medical term of *medulla oblongata* and sometimes . . . . (7) simply the hindbrain. This is the sort of brain found in some very . . . . (8) animals that possess a spinal cord of any sort. . . . . (9) next to the hindbrain in humans and more advanced types of animals with a spinal cord is a . . . . (10) of brain tissue known as the *cerebellum*, or little brain.

Now complete the labelling of the diagram above by filling in a) and b).

c 1 Why does the writer use the words 'might' and 'apparently'?
   2 Why does the writer use the words 'identified', 'known' and 'called'?
   3 Could the writer have avoided the repetition of 'sort'?

3 Reading

Prediction

a Do you think the following are true (T) or false (F)?
   1 Worms do not have brains.
   2 Horses are 'intelligent'.
   3 Dolphins are 'intelligent'.
   4 An animal which has had its brain removed dies immediately.

b Now check your answers with the following text.

The primitive areas of the brain still control certain basic functions in humans, just as they do in simple
5 animals such as worms. The reflex action that occurs when a person touches a hot stove is, for practical purposes, identical with
10 the reaction of a worm to an environmental threat.
     Later in the scale of evolution, the brain acquired the functions
15 necessary for survival as a fish or reptile. Eventually, the brain of mammals evolved with an over-growth of nervous tissue
20 that became the cerebrum, with its still later developing cerebral cortex that covers the primitive basal brain structures. In
25 some lower animals and in an unborn human child, the cerebral portion of the brain is smooth. But as the brain grows the cerebral
30 cortex becomes folded and convoluted in order to accommodate a greater surface area. The brain surfaces of other
35 'intelligent' animals such as the horse and dolphin have similar convolutions.
     The muscles of the head and neck area, like those of
40 other parts of the body, can be thought of as slaves of the central nervous system, which has more than one level of
45 command. The lower level of command, in the old primitive area, sends orders along the nervous pathways ordering the
50 muscles to react in a primitive manner to a contact with the environment. The higher command post, in the
55 cerebral cortex, handles muscle activities that depend in part on the will of the mind. Scientists learned in the 19th century
60 that animals with the cerebral cortex removed surgically continued to live but functioned at a primitive level with their
65 basal brains.

Text-attack skills

c 1 Underline all the time expressions in lines 1–10 of the text **3b**, for example, <u>still</u> (line 2).

2 Insert the following link words into the paragraphs indicated and make any other changes necessary to produce correct sentences.
  a) For example (para. 1)   e) On the one hand (para. 3)
  b) however (para. 2)   f) on the other (para. 3)
  c) Similarly (para. 2)   g) As a result (para. 3)
  d) In fact (para. 3)

d Notice how vocabulary also connects the different parts of the text by similarity or contrast of meaning:

'Primitive' (line 1) connects with 'basic' (line 3) and 'simple' (line 4). 'Smooth' (line 28) contrasts with 'folded' (line 30).

Now look back at the text and find these connecting words.

1 'Reflex action' (line 6) connects with . . . . (line . . .).
2 'Evolution' (line 13) connects with . . . . (line . . .) and . . . . (line . . .).
3 'Convoluted' (line 31) connects with . . . . (line . . .).
4 'The lower level of command' (line 46) contrasts with . . . . (line . . .).
5 'Command' (line 45) connects with . . . . (line . . .).
6 'Primitive manner' (line 51) contrasts with . . . . (line . . .) and connects with . . . . (line . . .).

e The following sentences continue the text in **3b** but are in the wrong order. Put them in the correct order (the first and last are done for you).

a) Thus, an injury to the motor cortex on the right side of the brain could result in paralysis or a similar loss of function on the left side of the body.

b) That is, the motor cortex, or portion of the cerebral cortex that controls motion, is situated on the left side of the brain.

c) The human brain is divided near the top into two, right and left symmetrical halves.

d) It is, however, responsible for muscle action on the right side of the body.

e) This relationship can be demonstrated by touching one of the motor cortex areas with an electrode, thus producing a muscle contraction in a particular area of the body.

f) Each of the two halves, in addition to certain individual responsibilities in the area of mental work, such as language, controls the movement of the body half on the opposite side.

g) There are areas of the motor cortex of the brain that correspond to particular parts of the body.

h) The relationship actually is much more specific.

i) And vice versa.

j) In this way, doctors can identify a motor area on the right side of the brain that will cause the muscles on a finger, leg, neck or another body area on the left side of the body to contract. (10)

How did you work out the correct order of the sentences? Underline all the words that helped you.

f Which of the sentences in **3e**

1 make a contrast?
2 express a result?
3 give more specific information?
4 include an example?
5 explain a previous point?

Underline the words or phrases that helped you.

4 Writing

The following passage is difficult to follow — it is really only a list of sentences. Rewrite it in three well-connected paragraphs. Use link words or phrases and make any other changes necessary.

The brain, like other essential organs, depends on a steady oxygen supply. A steady oxygen supply ensures the brain's continuous function. The brain's main nutritional substance is glucose. The brain is very sensitive to changes in the blood glucose level. If a diabetic receives an overdose of insulin there is a fall in the blood sugar. If there is a fall in the blood sugar the brain's activity is disturbed. There is loss of consciousness. It is important to understand the functions of the different parts of the brain. It is important in many fields of human activity. Brain surgery in the treatment of Parkinson's disease is very effective. Surgeons know exactly where to cut the affected brain part. A child's difficulties in learning to read can be shown to arise from misinterpretation of visual impulses. Or an emotional block to learning. Or the cortex fails to develop. And some children have difficulty in speaking. We can understand the brain. The brain is the seat of intelligence. Man has attained greater self-knowledge.

UNIT 23 MAESTRO

1 Speaking

Listen to the extract from a famous symphony and then answer the following questions.

1 Is it modern?

2 Do you like it?

Describe your feelings about the music; you may want to use the following adjectives:

Like

BRILLIANT PROFOUND

LOVELY GRAND

Cheerful graceful

Dislike

dull DIFFICULT

Old Fashioned

MONOTONOUS

superficial

depressing

2 Reading

Jigsaw reading

a In pairs, one of you read text **G** on page 201 and the other, text **H** on page 202. Try to complete as much of the table as you can.

	Text G	Text H
Born (place)		
Worked for		
Early life		
Character		
Left Salzburg (when)		
Influences on his music		
How he wrote music		
Style of his works		
Works mentioned and when written	1 2 3 4	1 2 3 4
Description of any of the works mentioned		
Died (place and age)		

b Compare information with your partner and complete any blanks in your table. Can you work out the dates of the composer's birth and death?

Vocabulary

c Can the adjectives in the table below be used to describe a person, a work of art (such as a piece of music) or both? Read the texts again and complete the table.

Adjective	People	Work of Art
1 immortal	...√...	....
2 great	...√...	...√...
3 unique	....	....
4 precocious	....	....
5 vast	....	....
6 effortless	....	....
7 consistent	....	....
8 symmetrical	....	....
9 expressive	....	....
10 instrumental	....	....
11 tragic	....	....
12 resounding	....	....
13 sensational	....	....
14 outspoken	....	....
15 superficial	....	....

3 Grammar Relative clauses

a Look at the following relative clauses:
a) Mozart, *who as a child prodigy was fêted everywhere*, was buried in a pauper's grave.
b) Composers *who write music for films* are highly paid.
1 Read the two sentences aloud. What is the difference between them?
2 Omit the clause beginning 'who' in each sentence – do the sentences still make sense?
3 Which of the two sentences gives us essential information in the relative clause?
4 Which of the two types of relative clause do you think is rare in speech. Why?
5 Which type of relative clause is separated off by commas in a written sentence? Why?

b Say whether the following sentences are correct or incorrect and give your reasons.
1 Wole Soyinka, who was born in Nigeria, won the Nobel Prize for literature in 1986.

2 The novels and plays, that Soyinka wrote about African society, have become modern classics.

3 Soyinka who was pleased that the prize had come to Africa is mainly a writer of plays.

4 The Nobel Prize which is awarded every year has been won by non-western writers only twice before.

5 His play *A Dance of the Forests*, which was first performed on Nigerian Independence Day in 1960, was a warning to the African nations not to repeat the mistakes of the past.

6 The play, that explores Nigeria's relationship with its past, presents Nigerian ancestors in a great ceremony celebrating Nigerian independence.

7 Soyinka, who writes in English, is considered, along with Lorca and Brecht, one of the great twentieth-century playwrights.

Wole Soyinka

Anita Desai

4 Writing

Pre-writing

a Below is some information on Anita Desai – use it to write a brief account of her life and work. Use relative clauses where appropriate.

Indian. Born 1937. Educated: Queen Mary's Higher Secondary School, Delhi. BA, Delhi University (English Literature) 1957. Married 1958. Four children.

First novel: *Cry the Peacock* (1963); heroine: daughter of a wealthy North Indian Brahmin – murders her husband at the end of the novel.

Second novel: *Voices in the City*; theme: life in Calcutta (1965); despair and suicide; characters: orthodox Hindu backgrounds – destroy themselves, go insane.

Fire on the Mountain written 1977; won awards, e.g. Winifred Holtby Prize; explores desolation of family group of lonely women; use of language – confident, sophisticated.

Free writing

b Now write about the life and works of a modern composer or writer who you think is very talented or even a genius!

UNIT 24 NOWHERE MAN

1 Speaking
   1 What do you think you will be doing in thirty, forty and fifty years time?
   2 Do you think you will have lived a free, happy life?
   3 Do you think you will have done anything to make you famous?
   4 Do you think you will be different from the average in any way?

2 Reading / Listening

   a To find out the answer to question 4 above, imagine you have died and an official is asking for information to add to some statistics. How would your family answer questions about you? Make a note of the answers you think they might give to the questions below (but do not fill in the boxes yet).

---

1 Was he/she ever fired?

   (a) Yes ☐ (b) No ☐

2 Did he/she ever go to war?

   (a) Yes ☐ (b) No ☐

3 Were his/her employers satisfied with him/her?

   (a) Yes ☐ (b) No ☐

4 Did he/she go on strike when fellow workers did?

   (a) Not always ☐ (b) Always ☐ (c) Never ☐

5 Did he/she ever disagree with what the majority of people thought?

   (a) Yes ☐ (b) No ☐

6 Did he/she enjoy a drink with friends?

   (a) Occasionally ☐ (b) Frequently ☐ (c) Never ☐

7 How often did he/she buy a newspaper?

   (a) Occasionally ☐ (b) Every day ☐

8 Did he/she complain about his/her children's education?

   (a) Yes ☐ (b) No ☐

---

   b Listen to the poem and fill in the questionnaire above for the person you hear about. Tick the appropriate box.

   c Compare the answers from the listening with your answers in **2a** – what do they suggest? Will you be an unknown citizen in thirty, forty or fifty years time?

3 Reading

a   Read the poem and check your completion of the questionnaire in **2b.**

> ### *The Unknown Citizen*
> *(To JS 07/378*
> *This Marble Monument*
> *is Erected by the State)*
>
> He was found by the Bureau of Statistics to be
> One against whom there was no official complaint,
> And all the reports on his conduct agree
> That, in the modern sense of an old-fashioned word, he was a saint,
> For in everything he did he served the Greater Community.
> Except for the War till the day he retired
> He worked in a factory and never got fired,
> But satisfied his employers, Fudge Motors Inc.
> Yet he wasn't a scab or odd in his views,
> For his Union reports that he paid his dues,
> (Our report on his Union shows it was sound)
> And our Social Psychology workers found
> That he was popular with his mates and liked a drink.
> The Press are convinced that he bought a paper every day
> And that his reactions to advertisements were normal in every way.
> Policies taken out in his name prove that he was fully insured,
> And his Health-card shows he was once in hospital but left it cured.
> Both Producers Research and High-Grade Living declare
> He was fully sensible to the advantages of the Instalment Plan
> And had everything necessary to the Modern Man,
> A phonograph, a radio, a car and a frigidaire.
> Our researchers into Public Opinion are content
> That he held the proper opinions for the time of year;
> When there was peace, he was for peace; when there was war, he went.
> He was married and added five children to the population,
> Which our Eugenist says was the right number for a parent of his generation,
> And our teachers report that he never interfered with their education.
> Was he free? Was he happy? The question is absurd:
> Had anything been wrong, we should certainly have heard.

b Discuss the following questions.

1 Who do you think is the speaker/writer of the poem?
   a) a teacher   b) a politician   c) a bureaucrat   d) other
2 Who is the 'he' of the poem?
3 Which of the following describe 'JS'?
   a) saintly   d) popular   g) free
   b) odd   e) happy   h) normal
   c) sound   f) healthy   i) patriotic

Appreciating style

c Look at the table below. Write 'F' or 'I' in the appropriate column depending on whether you would usually find the word in a formal written context (F), or in an informal spoken context (I). The 'synonyms' in the final column below may help you decide.

	F/I	Synonyms
1 erect	....	put up, build
2 conduct	....	behaviour
3 fire (V)	....	dismiss, sack
4 scab	....	'blackleg'*
5 odd	....	strange
6 report (V)	....	say, state
7 declare	....	say, state
8 mate	....	friend
9 proper	....	right
10 paper	....	newspaper

d Look at the following sentences.

1 Grade them 1–10. (1 = very informal, 5 = neutral, 10 = very formal)

1–10

a) This marble monument is erected by the State. ☐
b) He was found by the Bureau of Statistics to be . . . ☐
c) . . . one against whom there was no official complaint. ☐
d) He never got fired. ☐
e) He was popular with his mates. ☐
f) He liked a drink. ☐
g) Had anything been wrong, we should certainly have heard. ☐
h) He wasn't a scab. ☐
i) When there was peace, he was for peace, when there was war, he went. ☐
j) He was fully sensible to the advantages of . . . ☐

* a worker who does not strike when his/her fellow workers do, or who is not a member of a union to which his/her colleagues all belong.

2 What makes the examples in 1 formal or informal? You may refer to both grammar and vocabulary.

3 What is the effect of this mixture of formal and informal elements in the poem?

4 Writing

Write an obituary of an unknown citizen in your country. Would he or she be like the citizen in the poem? What are the modern qualities of an unknown citizen? Use the past tense and include some passives.

Example:

He was found to be perfectly normal in every way; he had a wife and two children; he believed in the necessity of the nuclear deterrent. All our reports agree that, in the age of the microchip, . . .

Include information about:

- his education; his job
- his reaction to official propaganda
- his material possessions (house, car, video, home computer)
- his attitude to space exploration, 'star wars', etc . . .

Extension six

a Place each word in one of the blanks below. Use each word once only.

correlation	outstanding	utterly	precocious
IQ	distinguished	gripping	reported
creative	masterpiece	provocative	conduct
consistently	triumph	phenomenal	
criteria	immensely	unique	

It is not surprising that as a child this novelist did well at school – she has a high . . . . (1). Her teachers . . . . (2) that she was very hard-working. She . . . . (3) produced good exam results, year after year. Because she was so young, many considered her . . . . (4) . But no one could ever complain of her . . . . (5), for she was always well-behaved.

Her first novel was considered to be a . . . . . . (6) . It combined a . . . . . . (7) story, with a . . . . (8) theme. And in fact it became a . . . . (9) best-seller. Her . . . . (10) talents were displayed even more clearly in her second novel. By whatever . . . . (11) you measured the book, it was better than her first. And it too became an . . . . . . (12) success. It was so successful, in fact, that it was made into a film, which was . . . . (13) popular.

Her parents had been very ordinary, which proved once again that there is no . . . . (14) between the ability of parents and their children. In any case, her parents were . . . . (15) delighted. They never expected to have such a . . . . (16) daughter. They considered her success a . . . . (17) for them all. Indeed, one might say she was . . . . (18).

b Rewrite the following sentences using *however, wherever, whoever, whatever*.

1 I don't care who the composer is; he has written an awful song.
2 I don't care how intelligent he is – Nick won't get through the exam in June.
3 It doesn't matter what kind of problem it is; we must find a solution.
4 We should try, where it is possible, to include a measure of creativity in intelligence tests.
5 Mozart was gifted, that's for sure, but he still died in poverty.

c Rewrite the following sentences using a relative clause.
1 I'm talking about a Mel Brooks film. We saw it last week.
2 This symphony is by Mozart – it's called the 'Jupiter'.
3 This ceiling was painted by Michelangelo. It is a masterpiece.
4 The Nobel prize for literature is awarded every year. Wole Soyinka won it in 1986.
5 This building is an impressive example of neo-classical architecture. It was built in the 19th century.

d Fill each of the numbered blanks with one suitable word.

Most ordinary people are .... (1) that the creative person is someone who is .... (2) with a certain quality that the rest of us do not .... (3). This conception is almost universally .... (4) by psychologists. The majority of psychologists have found that all individuals to some .... (5) possess all abilities, except in pathological cases. .... (6) acts can therefore be expected of all individuals, ... (7) feeble or however infrequent those acts may be. .... (8) the nature of creative talent, those persons who are .... (9) as creative merely have more of what all of us have to some .... (10). Of course, ... (11) may be something only a few people seem to have, but on closer investigation it seems .... (12) that what most people are content to call 'inspiration' is the realization of what psychologists believe is available to all. Except for rare cases, such as that of Mozart, who was a child .... (13) and does indeed seem to have been unquestionably gifted with 'inspiration', every person with some degree of .... (14) will benefit from a good education and a stimulating environment. The role the family plays in the shaping of personality, the sensitivity and adventurousness which are encouraged by parents and teachers will all .... (15) the nature of intelligence and creativity.

Nevertheless, psychologists seem to be convinced that we cannot explain what it is that makes for .... (16) ability in creative work. We do not know enough about the .... (17) personality to say what distinguishes a .... (18) from, for example, an outstanding performer or just someone with creative ability. We do know that however gifted, most outstanding people need training and other assistance in order to fulfil their potential. .... (19) skilled, geniuses need the opportunity to practise; however .... (20), their inspiration has to be recognized, as Mozart's was by Haydn, and it has to be stimulated and directed. What .... (21) the great artist or thinker is the opportunity he or she is given to produce work of a .... (22) high standard. Mozart's genius seems to lie in the effortless .... (23) of consistently brilliant work. To what extent, though, was this made possible by the early .... (24) of his genius by his father, who showed him off throughout Europe as a .... (25) prodigy?

7
On the dark side

1 Speaking

a Look at the following pictures. Together they tell a story. Can you guess what the story is about?

b Which of the following sentences might occur in a story based on the pictures in **1a**? Give your reasons.

1 I cannot say how the idea first came to me – but it soon haunted me day and night.
2 He said to himself, 'It is nothing but the wind in the trees – go to sleep.'
3 For a second the doctor sat in total darkness, surrounded by silence.
4 He listened, dumbstruck; he couldn't believe his ears. She had been dead for years, and yet ...
5 There was only one light on, right at the top of the house, in the attic where she had been living before that night when ...

2 Listening / Speaking

a You are going to hear the sequence of sounds listed below (1–12). The 'sounds' are in the correct order, but the 'causes' are in the wrong order. Put the causes in the correct order by numbering them 1–12 (the first one is done for you).

Sound	Cause	
1 crashing	rain	. . .
2 drumming	a car	. . .
3 howling	glass	. . .
4 screeching	a door	. . .
5 crashing	footsteps	. . .
6 tinkling	someone	. . .
7 slamming	a gate	. . .
8 crunching	a dog	. . .
9 whistling	thunder	**1.**
10 gasping	the wind	. . .
11 creaking	tyres	. . .
12 barking	the wind	. . .

b Listen again to each sound and describe what you hear like this:
*That sounds like **the crashing of thunder**.*
*That must be **the wind howling**.*
– and if you're not sure what the sound is:
*That could be/might be **the tinkling of glass**.*

Prediction

c The sounds you have heard tell a story. Guess the following.
1 Where does the story take place?
2 When does the story take place?
3 How many people are involved in the story?

3 Listening

Gist listening

a Now listen to the actual story and check your guesses. Were you right?

Locating specific information

b Listen again and fill in the blanks in the following text.

> The thunder was right overhead now and the rain . . . . . . (1) on the car roof, was like a solid black curtain between Dr Macbird and the night. It was hypnotic: where was he? The only answer came from the wind . . . . . . (2) in the trees. The voice on the phone had been . . . . . . (3), almost hysterical: 'Doctor, come quickly. Please come quickly.'
>
> Suddenly, no more than ten yards in front of the car, Dr Macbird saw three dark figures . . . . . . (4) in the middle of the road. He braked violently. The tyres screeched as the car skidded uncontrollably towards the edge of the road and, with a crash and a tinkle of . . . . . . (5) glass, smashed into a tree.
>
> For a second the doctor sat in total darkness, surrounded by silence. He muttered a curse, sighed, then he got out and slammed the door. It was then that he suddenly felt afraid. Had he really seen those human figures or had they been the shadows of trees, their branches . . . . . . (6) like living things in the wind?
>
> Slowly, he walked forward. He could see nothing but the dim outline of the trees against the sky and he could hear only his own footsteps . . . . . . (7) on the road and the wind . . . . . . (8) in the trees. Suddenly, he gasped. What was that? Yes, surely there was someone ahead of him, just . . . . . . (9) off the road. The doctor approached the spot and saw a gate and the shape of a large house . . . . . . (10) some distance back from the road. As he opened the gate it creaked loudly and a dog barked in the distance.

c How do you think the story will continue? In groups, discuss the following possibilities.
  1 Dr Macbird finds his patient dead and hears mysterious sounds in the house.
  2 Dr Macbird finds his patient transformed into a monster of some kind.
  3 Dr Macbird finds his patient drinking a cup of tea and watching television.
  4 Dr Macbird enters the house, the door slams behind him and he hears a bat flying in through the window.

d Do you like ghost stories? Why? Why not?

Appreciating style

e   Look at the following structure from the text:
a) ... the rain, **drumming** on the car roof, was like ...
Compare:
b) ... The rain **was drumming** on the car roof. **It was** like ...
c) ... the rain, **which was drumming** on the car roof, was like ...
Why does the writer use structure a) rather than b) or c)?

Now rewrite the following like a) above.
Example:
Three dark figures were standing in the road. They started to move towards him.
► *Three dark figures, standing in the road, started to move towards him.*
1   The doctor was beginning to feel afraid. He turned round.
2   The wind gave the only answer. It was howling in the trees.
3   The car, which was skidding violently, went out of control and hit a tree.
4   The shadows of the trees swayed like living things; they made him want to turn back.
5   His footsteps crunched on the road; they echoed in the silence.
6   The wind whistled in the trees; it reminded him that he was alone.

4 Writing

Here are some notes about how the story continues. Write the rest of the story using the *-ing* form of the verb where appropriate. Provide your own ending to the story.

He reached the house ...
House almost in darkness, silence.
Light shining in one window – someone in the house.
Upstairs, voices murmuring.
Woman's voice, wailing in sorrow or pain?
Walk upstairs. Floorboards creak. Someone coming?
Silence again. Fear.
Light shining through keyhole – someone inside.
Hears laughter, moaning, sobbing.
Looks through keyhole and sees ...

UNIT 26 DO YOU BELIEVE IN ...?

1 Reading / Speaking

Prediction

a In this section you are going to read about witches. Which of the following words do you think might occur in the reading texts? Give reasons for your choice.

	Text A	Text B	Line
1 magic	. . .	. . .	. . . .
2 spell	. . .	. . .	. . . .
3 weird	. . .	. . .	. . . .
4 charm	. . .	. . .	. . . .
5 cat	. . .	. . .	. . . .
6 dog	. . .	. . .	. . . .
7 orgy	. . .	. . .	. . . .

b In pairs, one of you read text **A** on page 197 and the other, text **B** on page 198.
Complete the table above by ticking (✓) the appropriate box and giving line references. Were you right about which words occurred?

Vocabulary

c Still in pairs, each read your own text and try to match the definitions below with the appropriate word from the box.
1 the day on which witches gathered to worship the devil
2 object with magical qualities
3 spirit disguised as an animal
4 a small community of witches
5 system of religious worship
6 wild party

> coven
> black sabbath
> charm
> cult
> orgy
> familiar

Now check with your partner to see if you have the same answers.

Note-taking

d In pairs, each take notes from one of the two texts to complete as much as possible of the table on the following page.

	Witches					
	Male or female	Rich or poor (social status)	How they spent their time	Pets or familiars	Distinguishing marks	Who believed in them
Text A						
Text B						

Now exchange information with your partner to fill any blank spaces in your table.

2 Listening

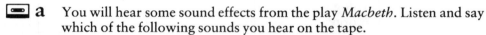 **a** You will hear some sound effects from the play *Macbeth*. Listen and say which of the following sounds you hear on the tape.

1 The wind howling   5 An owl hooting
2 The crashing of thunder   6 A drum beating
3 A cat miaowing   7 The wind whistling
4 A dog barking

b Listen to the extract from the play and answer the following questions.

1 What can you guess about the first three speakers'
   a) identity?
   b) age and appearance?
   c) movements?
2 Where do you think the scene takes place?
3 Who or what do you think Graymalkin and Paddock are?

c Listen to the extract again and complete the gaps with a word that rhymes with the last word in the previous line (the first is done for you as an example).

First witch	When shall we three meet again
	In thunder, lightning, or in *rain*?
Second witch	When the hurly burly's done
	When the battle's lost and . . . . (1)
Third witch	That will be ere the set of . . . . (2)
First witch	Where the place?
Second witch	Upon the heath.
Third witch	There to meet with Macbeth.

First witch	I come, Graymalkin!
Second witch	Paddock calls.
Third witch	Anon.
All	Fair is foul, and foul is fair:
	Hover through the fog and filthy . . . . (3)
	[Later]
Third witch	A drum! a drum!
	Macbeth doth . . . . (4)
All	The weird sisters, hand in hand,
	Posters of the sea and . . . . (5)
	Thus do go about, about:
	Thrice to thine, and thrice to mine,
	And thrice again, to make up . . . . (6)
	Peace! The charm's wound up.

Vocabulary

d What do the following words from the above extract have in common?
ere   anon   doth   thine

e Now underline the words or structures in the following extract which are no longer used in modern English.

Macbeth	So foul and fair a day I have not seen.
Banquo	How far is't called to Forres? What are these
	So withered and so wild in their attire,
	That look not like th' inhabitants o' the earth
	And yet are on't. Live you? Or are you aught
	That man may question? You seem to
	understand me,
	By each at once her choppy finger laying
	Upon her skinny lips: you should be women,
	And yet your beards forbid me to interpret
	That you are so.

f Can you guess the modern equivalents of the following Elizabethan
words used in the extracts?

1 ere	3 doth	5 attire	7 choppy
2 anon	4 thrice	6 aught	8 thine

3 Reading / Speaking

Note-taking

a Compare the text from *Macbeth* with the texts on witches in **1b**. What
differences and similarities are there in the information they give us about
witches? Make notes on the following topics and compare your answers.

Magic   Sex   Animals   Appearance   Age   Distinguishing marks

Role-play

b You are going to conduct the trial of Macbeth. Before you do, read this
summary of the plot so far ...

After defeating an army of Norwegian and Scottish rebels, Macbeth and
Banquo, generals in Duncan, King of Scotland's army, meet three witches
on a heath. The witches prophesy that Macbeth shall be Thane of Cawdor
and later King, and that Banquo will be the father of kings. Immediately
afterwards comes the news that Macbeth has been created Thane of
Cawdor. Macbeth describes these events in a letter to Lady Macbeth, his
wife, and when she hears that Duncan is coming to stay in their castle, she
decides that the King must be dealt with.

Macbeth, stimulated by the witches' words and his own ambition, is
persuaded by Lady Macbeth to kill the sleeping King. Duncan's sons,
Malcolm and Donalbain are suspected of the murder. They escape and
Macbeth is crowned King. Macbeth now acts alone and he tries to frustrate
the fulfilment of the prophecy concerning Banquo by arranging the murder
of Banquo and his son. However, Banquo's son escapes. Haunted by the
ghost of Banquo, Macbeth consults the three witches who tell him to beware
of Macduff, the Thane of Fife; that no one born of woman has the power to
harm him; and that he will never be defeated till Birnam Wood comes to
Dunsinane. Learning that Macduff has joined Malcolm in England, Macbeth
orders the murder of Lady Macduff and her children. Then, deserted by
his friends, he awaits the attack of his Scottish enemies and their English
allies ...

At this point we leave Shakespeare and bring Macbeth and the three
witches to trial. Macbeth is charged with murder; the witches with
incitement to murder.

Now role play the trial of Macbeth.

Stage 1
Witnesses prepare their evidence.
Judge, Jury, Prosecution and Defence study the case (the plot and characters in the play *Macbeth*).

Stage 2
Witnesses are examined by Prosecution and Defence.

Stage 3
The Jury arrives at a verdict and, if the verdict is 'guilty', a sentence.

Role cards

Macbeth
A brave soldier and until the murder of Duncan, a loyal subject. Sensitive, eloquent, ambitious; wants to prove to his wife that he is not a coward . . . Believes in the supernatural and during the trial will try to blame everything on his wife and the witches. Reads science fiction novels and never misses a Steven Spielberg movie.

The Three Witches
Believe that in time of war witches play an important role in giving people hope and a belief in the future. They are very professional and try to tell the truth and give sound advice. They claim they are not witches but counsellors, futurologists using scientific methods. They quarrel a lot and can't agree on the exact wording of their prophecies.

Macduff
His family was slaughtered by Macbeth's agents as a result of the witches' advice. As he was born by Caesarean section and 'not born of woman' he could fulfil the witches' prophecy. Believes Macbeth was motivated by cruelty and lust for power and that witchcraft is just an excuse. Strongly opposed to tyranny.

Lady Macbeth
Believes you've got to get on in life. She has no children and gets bored with keeping the palace tidy. Feels she is as good as any man in matters of administration and that women should go into politics more and assert their rights. Dislikes cowardice and wants her husband to fulfil his potential. Does not believe in witchcraft herself but feels it has helped her husband realize his potential.

The Judge
Prepare yourself by finding out as much about the play *Macbeth* as possible. Consult the plot summary and take notes.

The Jury
Prepare yourselves by finding out as much as you can about the play *Macbeth*. Consult the plot summary and take notes.

Malcolm
Elder son of Duncan and heir to the throne. Sleeping next door to his father on the night of the murder. Woken by Macduff; suspected Macbeth immediately, and fled. Likes tennis and fast cars. Tends to order people around (including his younger brother, who is jealous of him). Hates politics but likes wearing a uniform. Orders his soldiers to cut down branches in Birnam Wood and march camouflaged to Dunsinane.

Donalbain
Younger son of Duncan and next in succession after Malcolm. Was sleeping next door to his father's bedroom on the night of the murder. Wants to become King; loves politics and never happy about Malcolm being heir. Saw books on witchcraft in Macbeth's library and heard Macbeth talking to himself about daggers just before the murder.

Prosecutor
You will try and prove that Macbeth murdered Duncan out of ambition spurred on by his wife and that the witches are tricksters, used by Macbeth as an excuse. You want the death penalty for Macbeth.

Defence Counsel
You will try and prove that although Macbeth is a murderer, there are extenuating circumstances, particularly his almost religious belief in the supernatural. You will try and prove that the witches were convincing and that anybody would have been deceived by them. Propose maximum five-year prison sentence.

4 Writing

a There was no trial in Shakespeare's play *Macbeth*. Using the information from the role cards, can you complete the summary of Shakespeare's plot? Check your completion with someone who knows the play or with a copy of the play itself.

b Write a plot summary like the one in **3b** for a book or play you have read.

UNIT 27 ON THE LIGHT SIDE

1 Speaking Imagine a visitor from outer space has arrived on earth.
In pairs, discuss:

1 What might the visitor look like?
2 How might the visitor have travelled to earth?
3 What might the purpose of the visit be?
   a) To collect samples of life on earth and take them back to the planet.
   b) To collect information for an invasion.
   c) To collect information in a guide book for other visitors, who might want to visit earth.
   d) To see how advanced or primitive life on earth is.

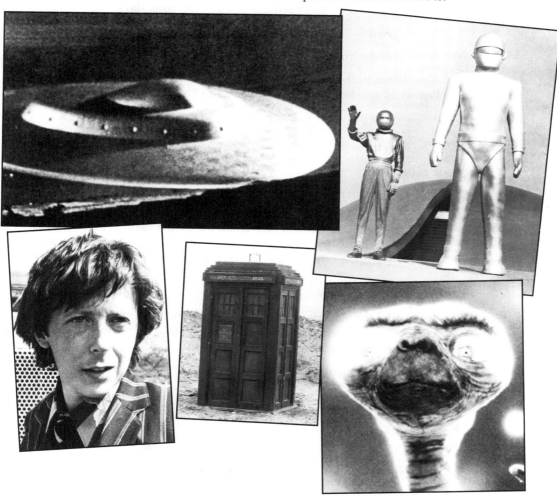

2 Listening

Locating specific information

a You will hear the visitor talking to a human.
Listen and see if you can find answers to any of the questions in **1**.

Intonation

b Listen again. The human repeats some of the words. Mark the direction of the voice on these repetitions (1–4).

↗ = up   1 'intended' ☐   3 'modulars' ☐
↘ = down 2 'teaser' ☐   4 'buzz them' ☐

Why does the human repeat these words in this way?

c Now listen to the next part of the tape and each time it stops, repeat the last word you hear in the same way as in **2b** above.

3 Reading

Prediction

a Below is the first sentence from a text which tells us more about the visitor. What sort of information do you think the text will contain?
'This friend of his had first arrived on the planet earth some fifteen earth-years previously, and he had worked hard to blend himself into earth society – with, it must be said, some success.'

Text-attack skills

b Now read the various paragraphs from the text and place them in the correct order. Underline the word or words that help you to do this. Were your predictions correct?

c Can you now answer all the questions in **1**?

A   'Green ones!' he would reply with a wicked grin, laugh wildly for a moment and then suddenly lunge for the nearest bar and buy an enormous round of drinks.
Evenings like this usually ended badly. Ford would get out of his skull on whisky, huddle into a corner with some girl and explain to her in slurred phrases that honestly the colour of the flying saucers didn't matter that much really.

B   He was not conspicuously tall, his features were striking but not conspicuously handsome. His hair was wiry and gingerish and brushed backwards from the temples. His skin seemed to be pulled backwards from the nose. There was something very slightly odd about him, but it was difficult to say what it was. Perhaps it was that his eyes didn't seem to blink often enough and when you talked to him for any length of time your eyes began involuntarily to water on his behalf. Perhaps it was that he smiled slightly too broadly and gave people the unnerving impression that he was about to go for their neck.

C   He struck most of the friends he had made on earth as an eccentric, but a harmless one – an unruly boozer with some oddish habits. For instance, he would often gatecrash university parties, get badly drunk and start making fun of any astrophysicists he could find till he got thrown out.

D   This friend of his had first arrived on the planet earth some fifteen earth-years previously and he had worked hard to blend himself into earth society – with, it must be said, some success. For instance he had spent those fifteen years pretending to be an out-of-work actor, which was plausible enough.

E   Thereafter, staggering semi-paralytic down the night streets he would often ask passing policemen if they knew the way to Betelgeuse. The policeman would usually say something like, 'Don't you think it's about time you went off home, sir?'

F   He had made one careless blunder though, because he had skimped a bit on his preparatory research. The information he had gathered had led him to choose the name 'Ford Prefect' as being nicely inconspicuous.

G   Ford wished that one would arrive soon because he knew how to flag flying saucers down and get lifts from them. He knew how to see the Marvels of the Universe for less than thirty Altairian dollars a day.

H   In fact, Ford Prefect was a roving researcher for that wholly remarkable book *The Hitch Hiker's Guide To The Galaxy*.

I   Sometimes he would get seized with oddly distracted moods and stare into the sky as if hypnotized until someone asked him what he was doing. Then he would start guiltily for a moment, relax and grin.
'Oh, just looking for flying saucers,' he would joke and everyone would laugh and ask him what sort of flying saucers he was looking for.

J   'I'm trying to, baby, I'm trying to,' is what Ford invariably replied on these occasions. In fact, what he was really looking for when he stared distractedly into the sky was any kind of flying saucer at all. The reason he said 'green' was that green was the traditional space livery of the Betelgeuse trading scouts. Ford Prefect was desperate that any flying saucer at all would arrive soon because fifteen years was a long time to get stranded anywhere, particularly somewhere as mind-bogglingly dull as the earth.

Vocabulary

d Give the grammatical category (e.g. noun, verb, etc.) of the following
words.

1 suspicion	3 suspicious	5 conspicuously
2 suspect	4 unsuspecting	6 inconspicuous

e Now place one of the words above into each of the following sentences.
1 His odd habits never made me . . . .
2 He was tall but not . . . . tall.
3 I never . . . . he was from another planet.
4 As he looked just like everybody else, he was . . . .
5 I hadn't the slightest . . . . he was from outer space.
6 He chose an . . . . human to tell his story to.

4 Grammar Past habits

a Look at these two sentences from the text. In which does *would* express
a past habit?
1 He *would* often ask policemen if they knew the way to Betelgeuse.
2 He wished that a flying saucer *would* arrive soon.

b Below are some more ways of expressing a past habit. In each case, what
is the correct form of the verb *ask*?
Example:
He kept on asking *policemen if they knew the way to Betelgeuse.*

1 He was always . . .		4 He frequently used to . . .
2 He had a habit of . . .		5 He was continually . . .
3 He was forever . . .		6 He would keep . . .

c Ford has now gone back to his planet. Look again at the text and list the
habits which might have told you Ford was from another planet. Practise
the dialogue below with your partner, referring to Ford's odd habits and
using the patterns in **4b** above.

Student A: I never dreamt he was from outer space.
Student B: What made me suspicious was that he was always . . .
Student A: True. He would keep . . .
Student B: But apart from that, he was plausible enough.

5 Speaking

Opposite is an extract from Ford's *Guide to Earth*. Decide in pairs
whether the 'strange behaviour' Ford describes is

1 cigarette smoking.	3 whistling.
2 kissing.	4 talking about the weather.

'I formed a theory to account for this strange behaviour. If humans don't keep exercising their lips, their mouths probably seize up. Later I abandoned this theory in favour of a new one. If they don't keep on exercising their lips, their brains start working. I have had to abandon this theory as well. I have decided I quite like humans after all, but I remain desperately worried about the terrible number of things they don't know.'

6 Writing

You have discovered your best friend who has just left earth was from the planet Betelgeuse. Write an account explaining why you had not previously suspected. Use the prompts below.

My friend had first arrived on earth some . . . years previously and had worked hard to blend into earth society.
For instance . . .
She/he made one careless blunder though, because . . .
She/he was not conspicuously . . .
Her/his features were . . .
There was something odd about her/him but . . .
Perhaps it was . . .
She/he struck most of our friends as . . .
For instance, she/he would often . . .
Sometimes, she/he would . . .
Also she/he would keep . . .
In fact, what she/he was really trying . . .

UNIT 28 AN INTERVIEW WITH FRANK

1 Speaking   In groups discuss these questions.
1 Who in the group likes horror films?
2 Why / Why not?
3 Who are some of the most famous characters from horror films?

2 Listening

Gist listening

a   Listen to the tape and find out:
1 How many people are talking?
2 Where are they?
3 What are they talking about?
4 Do you recognize any of them?

Note-taking

b   What is said about the neighbours and their habits? Listen again and take notes under the following headings.
1 The house next door
2 The house opposite
3 The house on the other side

c In pairs, compare your notes and see if you can work out who these people could be.

3 Grammar Emphatic position

a It is quite common in informal speech to place a word or phrase at the beginning of an utterance to give it special prominence.

Instead of saying:

	1	2
Instead of saying:	He said his name was	Ford

	2	1
You can say:		

Practise making similar sentences by correctly matching items from the left-hand column (1–5) with those in the right-hand column (a–e).

1 Fifteen years   a) he was.
2 Prefect   b) he always wore.
3 Very moody   c) he'd been on this planet.
4 Modulars   d) he said his name was.
5 Odd-shaped boots   e) he used to call them.

b It is also possible in informal speech to add a tag statement to an utterance for emphasis or explicitness, for example:

*That's a lot of nonsense, **that is**.*
*He talks a lot about flying saucers, **Ford does**.*

Practise adding tag statements with your partner.
Example: Ford / drink a lot?
▶ Student A: *Does Ford drink a lot?*
   Student B: *Oh yes, he drinks a lot, **Ford does**.*

1 Ford / always staring into space?
2 Ford / talk a lot about flying saucers?
3 Frankenstein / is a real monster?
4 Frankenstein / have strange neighbours?
5 The three old girls / talk in rhymes?
6 Ford / seem fairly normal?
7 Ford / been here a long time?
8 Ford / would like to go home?

c Listen to the interview with Frankenstein again and note down examples of the patterns practised in **3a** and **3b**.

d Look at this formal newspaper report of the interview and rewrite it to produce an informal dialogue. Use the patterns in **3a** and **3b** when you can (not in every sentence!).

> **In an interview last night Mr Frankenstein was questioned about the harmful effects of horror movies on teenagers.**
> He felt that such effects were often exaggerated, and claimed that other types of film were far more dangerous for young people. When asked to prove this, he pointed out that horror films were often set in unreal situations and were clearly not to be taken seriously. In contrast, he claimed that films showing violent crime were often set in everyday life, and were therefore more damaging. He also made the point that he was a fun-loving family man who did a lot of work for charity.
> A spokesperson for films of violent crime was not available for comment.

Begin like this:
Interviewer: *Don't your films harm teenagers?*
Frank: *That's exaggerating a bit, that is.*

4 Writing

Imagine you are a resident in the same street as Frankenstein; you heard the interview on TV and read the review in the newspaper. You are furious and want to tell your side of the story – you want the public to know what **really** goes on. Write a letter to the newspaper. Begin like this:

Dear Sir,

As one of Mr. Frankenstein's neighbours I would like to take issue with some of the outrageous things he said during the interview which went out on ABC Radio last Tuesday.

- Comment on his claim that he is not a monster.
- Disagree with his view of horror films.
- Give an example of an unpleasant scene from a 'Frankenstein' film.
- Comment on his strange appearance.
- Describe how you feel about your street being full of strange characters.
- Demand that something be done about it.

Extension seven

a   Fill each of the numbered blanks in the following passage with one suitable word.

Dear Roger,

I must tell you about the most awful dream I had the other night. Actually, it wasn't a dream, it was more of a . . . . (1). You know I don't believe in the . . . . (2): ghosts, witchcraft and all that, but what happened was so real, I'm actually beginning to . . . . (3) there must be some truth in it.

It was a terrible night, what with the wind . . . . (4) and the thunder . . . . (5) but finally I managed to get to sleep. . . . . (6) happened next was really frightening. There, at the end of the bed, stood a dark figure. I'm not . . . . (7) – honestly I could really see it. It was dark in the room, of course, but I saw the . . . . (8) of the figure clearly. I know not all ghosts are dangerous, but this one looked really . . . . (9). Then it spoke. At least, it made some sounds; it was . . . . (10), as if in pain.

You can imagine by this time I was trembling . . . . (11) Hiding under the blankets, I was . . . . (12) from head to foot. What terrified me . . . . (13) the thought that the thing might touch me. I knew if it did, I . . . . (14) scream. It kept on . . . . (15) strange sounds which now sounded more like curses or . . . . (16). Was it some kind of . . . . (17), sent to work its magic on me, I . . . . (18). Then it vanished into the wall.

. . . . (19) I fell asleep again is still a mystery to me. What do you make of it all? You know I was never . . . . (20) but now I'm not sure.

b   Match the item in the left-hand column with any sound-word you associate with it (the first one is done as an example for you).

SOUND ⟍ CAUSE	gasp	howl	screech	crash	crunch	tinkle	creak	sigh	whistle
wind		✓						✓	✓
bed									
tyres									
owl									
floorboards									
bells									
glass									
wolf									
thunder									
bones									
laughter									
breeze									
footsteps									
man / woman									

c Look at these sentences from the texts in unit 26.
a) *That witchcraft was common in the Middle Ages is not surprising.*
b) *It is surprising that witchcraft was common in the 16th century.*

Now make two sentences like a) or b) for the following.
1 There is no evidence to suggest the existence of witchcraft; this is disappointing.
  ▶ *That ...*
  ▶ *It is ...*
2 The first law making witchcraft an offence punishable by death was not passed until 1603; this is surprising.
3 Frankenstein can't stand horror films, which is very odd.
4 Dr Macbird set off alone in the middle of the night, which is strange.
5 Nobody recognized Ford Prefect, which is incredible.

d Fill the blanks in the following sentences with one of the following words.

inconspicuous	crashed	gasped	wailing
weird	imagine	cult	harmless
strike	moaning	charm	nonsense
plausible	unsuspecting	horror	

1 Last night I went to see one of those .... films.
2 It was about a monster that fell in love with an .... village girl – it followed her everywhere but she never realized.
3 This did not seem to .... anyone in the audience as odd.
4 But I must say I did not find it at all ....
5 After all, a monster is hardly an .... object.
6 The girl was a little .... as well, because she spent most of her time looking after her grandmother, who was a sort of a witch.
7 She was always collecting strange animals in the forest, so that Granny could make a new ....
8 The dramatic climax came when the monster, who had run off with the girl, was cornered by a group of witches. I must admit even I .... at the sight of them all.
9 To save you the trouble of going to see it, let me tell you that the monster finally .... to the ground from the top of a mountain.
10 The audience loved it, but I still don't understand why such films have become almost a ....
11 I can't .... why they are so popular.
12 They seem to me to be just a lot of ....
13 But I suppose they are at least fairly ....
14 No one could really be frightened by the sound of these witches ....
15 In fact, I felt quite sorry for the monster as he lay .... in pain at the end.

8
Do it yourself

UNIT 29   DOING THINGS WITH WORDS

1 Listening

a You will hear four speakers. Match each person you hear with one of the following by putting the appropriate number in the correct box.

a priest ☐   a policeman ☐   a father ☐
a child ☐   a customer ☐   a sinner ☐
a politician ☐   a would-be husband ☐
a motorist ☐   a car salesman ☐

b What is each speaker trying to do? Who do you think they are talking to?

2 Reading

Locating specific information

a Look at the pictures and read the text overleaf. Which situation mentioned in the text does each picture illustrate?

Persuasion is the art, primarily verbal, by which you get somebody to do what you want and make him, at the same time, think that this is what he had

5 wanted to do all the time.

It may be objected that the person persuaded – the persuadee, shall we call him? – may not be persuaded actually to 'do' anything, but merely to

10 accept an opinion or adopt an attitude. Within certain limits this objection is reasonable, but there is no clear-cut line between belief, attitude, and feeling on the one side, and an action on the

15 other. Furthermore, as soon as we look at the characteristic occasions on which persuasion takes place, we see that the process is usually targeted, at short or long range, toward action. You

20 persuade your friend to lend you five dollars until Saturday, you persuade the child to be good and go to bed, you persuade the policeman not to give you the ticket, you persuade the prospective

25 customer to buy the car, you persuade the sinner to repent and join the church, you persuade the girl to marry you, you persuade the voter to vote for you.

The persuader wants something that

30 can be granted by the persuadee, and if he is successful, it is granted and the persuadee is happy in the granting. Persuasion is the 'engineering of consent'. It is a way of exercising power

35 without creating resentment.

Persuasion represents power. Perhaps the highest compliment ever paid to the power of oratory, the prime form of persuasion in the world of Ancient

40 Greece and Rome, is embodied in the story of the death of Cicero. After Mark Antony had caused Cicero to be assassinated, and his head and hands were exposed in the Forum, Fulvia,

45 Antony's wife, stuck a gold pin through the tongue of the dead man to take vengeance on its power.

In that world oratory was the instrument that swayed the Athenian

50 electorate, the Senate of Republican Rome, or the street mob of the Roman Empire. Up to a few generations ago, even in this country, the ambitious young man studied his Greek and Latin,

55 and the halls of Congress rang with speeches imitated from Demosthenes or Cicero.

If the desire for power was once the spur that drove the young American to

60 a study of the classics, it still remains the fundamental motive for the exercise of persuasion. In that earlier and less sophisticated America, the occasions of public persuasion – the sermon, the

65 college oration, the speech on the hustings, the newspaper editorial, the debate in the state house or in the Capitol at Washington – were not numerous. Today such occasions are

70 multiplied a thousandfold, but numerous as they are, they are lost in the more massive manifestations of persuasion that pour from printing presses, crowd the television screen, fill the airwaves,

75 and blot out the landscape as our automobiles whirl down the highways. Demosthenes and Cicero have been replaced as the masters of persuasion by courses in salesmanship and psychology,

80 and other implementations of Dale Carnegie's famous formula *How to Win Friends and Influence People*.

The engineering of consent is central to our democratic, industrial society. We

85 live in the age of the advertising man, propaganda expert, and motivation analyst. What was once a limited exercise is now incessant and universal, and the stakes played for go higher

90 every day. The political, psychological, social, and moral consequences are not yet fully clear. Even so, some observers are beginning to feel that there is serious cause for concern that the

95 responsible forms of persuasion will be driven out by the irresponsible. That, however, is a question we shall come to later.

Text-attack skills

b   What do the following refer to?

1 this (line 4)   5 this country (line 53)
2 this objection (line 11)   6 such occasions (line 69)
3 he (line 31)   7 that (line 96)
4 that world (line 48)

Vocabulary

c   Discuss which of the four alternatives (a–d) is closest in meaning to the
    following words from the text.

1 'engineering' (line 33) means
   a) machinery b) achieving c) building d) creating
2 'oratory' (line 38) means a kind of
   a) power b) writing c) speaking d) flattery
3 'swayed' (line 49) means
   a) persuaded b) moved c) shouted at d) influenced
4 'spur' (line 59) means
   a) reason b) motive c) attitude d) action
5 'manifestations' (line 72) means
   a) demonstrations b) protests c) expressions d) forms

3 Speaking

a   Discuss how you would persuade

1 a child to go to bed.
2 a policeman not to give you a parking ticket.
3 someone to buy your twenty-year-old bicycle.
4 someone to marry you.

b   Which of the situations above could be expressed beginning with the
    following words? Complete the sentences as persuasively as you can.

1 There's something . . .   5 Now, come on . . .
2 Did I ever . . .   6 Look, I've got . . .
3 Don't you think . . .   7 I feel . . .
4 I'm sorry . . .   8 Why don't you . . .

c   In pairs, act out the following scenes.

1 A tries to borrow some money from B who is very mean!
2 A tries to persuade B, who is not very interested, to join his/her church/
   political party/pressure group.

4 Writing

Pre-writing

a The sentences below discuss the 'question' referred to at the end of the text in **2a**. Look back at the last paragraph before putting these sentences in the correct order (the first and last are done for you).

  a) The second view holds that persuasion is directed towards ends. According to this line of thought it can be used for good or ill and is therefore responsible for its ends. ☐

  b) The former relates to the effects on society of different kinds of persuasion. ☐

  c) The first holds that persuasion is merely a matter of technique. It is like, say, the power of nuclear energy: neutral in itself. ☐

  d) Let us look at these perspectives in more detail. **7**

  e) While the latter involves the individual's use of persuasion. ☐

  f) The particular question of ethics in persuasion depends on the relation of ends and means. Here we encounter two extreme views. **1**

  g) In addition to these two views we need to take account of another pair of perspectives: the social and the personal. ☐

b Underline all the words and phrases which helped you decide the correct order.

Free writing

c How do the kinds of persuasion referred to in the text in **2a** affect you personally? What effect do you think they have on society in general? Write an essay on 'The effect of mass media on society and the individual.'

UNIT 30 GETTING PEOPLE TO DO THINGS

1 Grammar Commands and suggestions

a Look at these ways of getting people to do things:

a) Listen!　　　c) You listen!
b) Do listen!　　d) Everyone listen!

Think of situations in which you might hear each of these. Which sound impolite? How can you make them sound more polite?

b Another way is to use *let*. This can be a command or suggestion, depending on who says it to whom. For example:

Let's finish the exercise.　　Let me have a look!

Note that *let us* has two forms in the negative:
Let's not arrive late.　　Don't let's arrive late.

Complete the sentences below with one of the following words:
somebody, you, yourself, us /'s, anyone, him

1 Don't let ... answer if he isn't sure.
2 Let ... not argue.
3 ... answer the phone.
4 Let ... who arrives late wait.
5 ... be quiet!
6 Behave ... !

c In pairs, match the words below to make commands or suggestions. Look at your column only; cover the other one. Take it in turns to read from your column. Then your partner must match up what you say with the correct word or phrase in his / her column.

Student A	Student B
1 you	a) me have a look
2 ——	b) close their books
3 don't	c) you eat any of that cake
4 be	d) be late
5 don't	e) not go out tonight
6 help	f) be punctual
7 let	g) run
8 let	h) let's go to the theatre
9 do it	i) yourself
10 somebody	j) go and tell him
11 everybody	k) have another drink
12 let	l) fair
13 don't	m) answer the phone
14 don't	n) let's argue
15 shall we go?	o) tell anyone
16 don't	p) anyone move
17 do	q) us try again
18 do	r) yes, let's
19 don't	s) each person say a few words
20 let's	t) yourself

2 Reading

a Here are some situations in which you might use the expression 'It's raining'. Can you think of any more?

b Read the following sentences and place them in the correct order to make a paragraph.

a) However, if we were to supply an appropriate context, we would readily show that the same form might equally serve as a suggestion or a refusal.

b) This is when the aim of the speaker is not so much to convey a piece of information as to establish a relationship with the person he is addressing.

c) Said by a mother whose child has just asked whether he can go and play in the garden, it means 'No, you can't'.

d) If we knew nothing of the context, we would imagine an utterance like 'It's raining' to be an example of the type of communication that is usually called *phatic communion*.

e) Talking about the weather is one way of doing this.

f) If it was addressed to somebody who was about to leave the front door of a house, it could have the meaning, 'I suggest that you take an umbrella or put on your raincoat'.

According to the text, what are three possible functions of the expression 'it's raining'?

c Which of the following best summarizes the paragraph?
  1 It is difficult to state what is the aim of a speaker.
  2 An individual sentence can be used to perform several different functions in the language.
  3 Phatic communion can be expressed in a variety of ways.
  4 'It's raining' is not a good example of the use of the present continuous tense.

3 Listening

Prediction

a Commands and suggestions are not the only way of getting people to do things. Which of the following could be used to get someone to close or open the door? Put a tick (√) in the first column.

	Your opinion	Tape
1 I wonder if you'd mind closing the door.	☐	☐
2 It's rather confidential, actually.	☐	☐
3 Were you born in a barn?	☐	☐
4 I think everybody's here.	☐	☐
5 It seems to be stuck.	☐	☐

b Now listen to the tape and complete the second column to see if you were right.

Inference

c Listen again and write notes for each of the five extracts to answer the questions 'where?' (i.e. what is the context or situation?) and 'who?' (i.e. who are the participants and what is their relationship?).

Where?	Who?
1	
2	
3	
4	
5	

4 Speaking

a Requests can also be made in several different ways. In pairs, discuss in which situation (1–4) you are most likely to hear which form of request (a–d). Why do you think this is so?

Situation	Request
1 Employee to boss	a) I wonder if I could possibly . . .
2 Wife to husband	b) Could I . . .
3 Neighbour to neighbour	c) I'm taking the car, OK?
4 Child to parent	d) I hope you won't mind my asking but . . .

b Discuss the following sentences (1–4) with your partner. Find as many functions for each sentence as possible, e.g. suggesting, inviting, requesting. Explain the situation in each case.

Sentence	Participants	Situation	Function
1 It's noisy in here.	*Teacher to students*	*Teacher wants students to be quiet*	*Giving a command*
2 I haven't seen you for ages.			
3 It's too expensive.			
4 I'm just going out.			

A "I haven't seen you for ages."

B "I'm just going out."

c Discuss with your partner what language you would use to
1 borrow a pen from a friend.
2 ask a neighbour to turn their music down.
3 borrow a friend's best coat.
4 ask a neighbour not to park outside your door or gate.
5 borrow a large sum of money from a member of your family.

d What have you learnt in these exercises about how to get people to do things?

5 Writing / Speaking

In groups, select one of sentences 1–5 below and write a dialogue to include that sentence so that it performs a function, e.g. giving a command, suggesting, persuading. Include at the beginning any necessary information about who the speakers are and where the dialogue takes place before reading it out to the class. Ask them to say what the function of your chosen sentence is.

> 1 *Did you say you got paid today?*
> 2 *There's a good film on at the Rex.*
> 3 *It's 4.30.*
> 4 *I've never been in an air balloon.*
> 5 *You look much nicer without a beard.*

Example:
Who: Two friends
Where: Outside a record shop

Bruce: Have you heard the new Rockers LP?
Arthur: No, I haven't. Is it as good as their first one?
Bruce: Yeah, I think so. I was going to buy it.
Arthur: Come on then. I'd love to hear it.
Bruce: It's a double album; a bit expensive.
Arthur: Yeah. Ridiculous, isn't it? We could take it round to Mary's and hear it there.
Bruce: Good idea. *Did you say you got paid today?*
Arthur: Are you broke again?
Bruce: What do you mean 'again'?
Arthur: OK. I'll lend you the money.

UNIT 31 GETTING PEOPLE TO BUY THINGS

1 Listening

▭ a Listen to the advertisement and answer the following questions.

1 What is the name of the product?
2 What kind of product is it?
3 Who is the advertisement aimed at?
4 Give six words used to describe the product.

a) ....   c) ....   e) ....
b) ....   d) ....   f) ....

▭ b Do you find the advertisement effective? Why? Why not?
Which of these alternative features would you expect to find in a successful advertisement? Why?

1 Simple words or complex words?
2 Familiar words or unfamiliar words?
3 Concrete words or abstract words?
4 Repetition or variety of vocabulary?

Listen again. Does the advertisement you have just heard have these features? Give examples.

2 Reading

a Fill in the gaps in the following text of the advertisement.

.... (1). So soft and .... (2) because it's the .... (3) toilet tissue that gives you .... (4) very special soothing .... (5), that .... (6) super softness. And only .... (7) gives you and your whole family .... (8) fresh, ... (9) feeling. They'll welcome the .... (10) of the softest .... (11) toilet tissue. Next time you shop, ask for .... (12) in any of five fresh colours.

Did you find it difficult to fill in the blanks? What does this tell you about the advertisement?

b Now read the following text and say which of the following criteria for a successful advertisement are discussed by the writer.

1 Selling power
2 Easy to remember
3 Attracts the readers'/listeners' attention
4 Easy to read or listen to

Whatever medium is used, advertising usually competes at a great disadvantage with other claims on the public's attention. The means of overcoming this disadvantage belong more often to other means of communication or to the transmission of language than to language itself: illustration, display typography, vocal emphasis, and so on. But one way of provoking the consumer's attention and curiosity is to present him with something surprising and unexpected, and this can be done as well by the unorthodox use of language as by other means. Any kind of unconventional behaviour, linguistic or otherwise, compels notice. The copywriter who exploits this fact can be compared to the legendary customer in a crowded restaurant, who stood on his head to attract the waiter's attention.

Departing from the conventions or rules of language can take many forms. In its grossest form, it is a violation of some obvious rule of the language: perhaps a 'wrong' spelling, or a grammatical solecism. Because this type of unorthodoxy usually carries penalties of misunderstanding or disapproval, it is the least important variety of unconventionality. Neologism (inventing new words) is another type which requires tactful handling. But there is considerable scope for inventiveness in the two areas of semantics and context. Semantic unorthodoxy can be crudely characterized as 'playing with the meanings of words', and is the basis of many linguistic jokes and some important literary devices such as metaphor and paradox. Contextual unorthodoxy consists in exploiting the incongruity of language in an inappropriate situation.

How to ensure that attentiveness continues after the bait has been taken? On a psychological plane, this might mean 'how to keep up suspense, interest, or amusement'. On a linguistic plane, it is more a question of how to make the message easy to grasp and assimilate. Some efforts have been made to assess objectively the 'readability' of written language, by measuring the simplicity of its structure in combination with other factors, or by finding out how easy it is to predict individual words from their environments.

The latter measure conflicts with attention value and interest value, which place a premium on the unexpected and enigmatic, as opposed to the predictable. But the conflict does not arise if, as often happens in press advertising, the surprise element is concentrated in the headline. 'Readability' has, unfortunately, no ready terminological equivalent for spoken language. However, the properties which make language easy to read are basically the same as those which make it easy to listen to. The basic requirements are a simple, personal, and colloquial style, and a familiar vocabulary.

C The writer mentions that the criteria of readability and attention value can conflict. Say whether the following features are characteristic of readability or attention value (or both). Tick (√) the appropriate column.

	Readability	Attention value
1 keeping up suspense	☐	☐
2 the text is easy to understand	☐	☐
3 the use of pictures, photographs	☐	☐
4 unusual use of language	☐	☐
5 simple grammar	☐	☐
6 surprising headline	☐	☐
7 everyday vocabulary	☐	☐
8 amusing content	☐	☐
9 visual effect of printed letters	☐	☐
10 personal style	☐	☐
11 playing with the meaning of words	☐	☐
12 making up new words	☐	☐

Vocabulary

d Using the prefixes given, change the words below to their opposite.

im- mis- dis- un- in-

Nouns	**Adjectives**
disadvantage	... appropriate
... attention	... conventional
... understanding	... orthodox
... approval	... personal
... congruity	... familiar
... fortune	... interested

e Replace the words in italics with words or phrases from the text which have a similar meaning.

1 Curiosity can be provoked by an *unorthodox* use of language.
2 As a *medium* of communication, advertising has many disadvantages compared with other claims on the public's attention.
3 *Neologism* is one *type* of linguistic unorthodoxy.
4 In its *crudest* form, departing from the conventions of the language consists in *breaking* some obvious rule.
5 Contextual unorthodoxy consists in *making use* of the incongruity of language in an inappropriate situation.

BEANZ MEANZ HEINZ

**From the people who invented civilization:
A more civilized way to fly**

**A MARS A DAY
HELPS YOU WORK,
REST AND PLAY**

3 Grammar *-ing* verb forms

a Look at this sentence from the text:

*Efforts have been made to assess the readability of written language by **measuring** the simplicity of its structure.*

Remember that the *-ing* form is used after all prepositions. In the examples below, rewrite the sentences using the phrases given, followed by *as* or one of these prepositions: *of, from, to, for.*

1 If they didn't spend so much on advertising, manufacturers could make their products cheaper.
Instead ...

2 Although they spend so much to advertise a new product, the manufacturer will not always succeed.
In spite ...

3 You may advertise your product extensively but you should also have done your market research carefully.
As well ...

4 You must know what the public wants and you must know how much they are prepared to pay.
Apart ...

5 Many products fail because companies misjudge the market.
As a result ...

6 Not only must you supply a good product but you also need a certain amount of luck.
In addition ...

7 There's little else you can do but keep your fingers crossed.
Except ...

8 They use advertising to increase their sales, they claim.
By means ...

b There are also a number of verbs which are followed by a preposition. In some cases the preposition is *to* and you may think this means it must be followed by the infinitive. But look at these examples:

I look forward to my journey across Europe.
I look forward to travelling across Europe.

Complete the following telephone conversation between two business executives, using the correct form of the words given.

look forward to	believe in	talk about
insist on	get round to	agree on

A: I finally .... (1) ringing you. Sorry it took so long.
B: That's OK. I just wanted to .... (2) making some changes in your proposal.
A: We could discuss it now on the phone, if you don't mind.
B: Well, I had hoped we'd be able to .... (3) having a meeting tomorrow.
A: It would be difficult but if you .... (4) us getting together ...
B: I .... (5) discussing these things thoroughly, so I think it's best.
A: OK. Tomorrow at nine in your office?
B: I .... (6) seeing you then.

c There are also a number of nouns followed by a preposition. Imagine you are copywriters. In pairs discuss the problems below and match them with the appropriate solution. Use the following nouns plus preposition in your discussion.

For example:

***One way of provoking** the consumer's attention is **by using** the unexpected or surprising.*

one method of	the difficulty in	a matter of
the idea of	one way of	a question of
the principle of		

Problem: How to ...

1 compete with other claims on the public's attention
2 provoke consumer's attention
3 present consumer with something surprising
4 depart from linguistic conventions
5 use semantics creatively
6 use context inventively
7 keep consumer's attention
8 assess readability
9 avoid conflict between predictability and attention value

Solution

a) concentrate surprise element in headline
b) use illustration, typography, vocal emphasis
c) measure the simplicity of sentence structure
d) create suspense
e) use the unexpected, surprising
f) violate obvious rule
g) exploit incongruity of language in the situation
h) use unorthodox language
i) play with meaning of words

4 Writing

Pre-writing

a How successful are the two advertisements opposite? Use the criteria listed in **2c** above to help you decide which of the two advertisements is more persuasive.

Free writing

b Write an advertisement for a holiday in your country — use as many of the techniques you have read about in this unit as you can.

Go Italy Go Citalia

GO FOR CHOICE, QUALITY AND STYLE

Italy is a world of wonderful holidays. Go for it with Citalia — no-one knows it better.

For the best of Italy, from top to toe, see Citalia's 244 page summer brochure. Then see Italy with Citalia. No-one offers so much choice, so much quality and imagination, so much style.

Air departures from London, Manchester and Glasgow. Special Train from London. Motoring holidays, too.

So go for the biggest and best. For all of Italy, pick up the Citalia summer brochure today.

say Si? to Citalia

ATOL 285 BCD

Mais Oui Help You?

You can see the Eiffel Tower from the white cliffs of Dover . . . with **Franglais Travels.**

Just hop on one of our **Franglais** luxury ferries connecting with a train service from Calais and you can be in the Champs-Elysées for lunch.

Franglais Travels is the simplest, fastest way to see the sights of Paris at an unbelievably low price.

So take a break — and enjoy *le weekend* French-style.

Write today for our brochure.

C'est magnifique, c'est Franglais!

UNIT 32 DOING AS YOU'RE TOLD

1 Speaking / Reading

a What do you know about skiing? Look at the skiers in the picture and see if you know which is the correct position for a beginner.

b Read the following text and check if you were right. Then using the text, find the beginner's faults in the other two skiers.

As a beginner you should start on relatively short skis, to make it easier to manoeuvre. Snowploughing is the first means of controlling your descents and your introduction to learning how to steer and skid the skis, so
5 it is vital that you learn how to do it properly. One of the difficulties you may have is developing the accuracy necessary to do a snowplough well.

The following is the ideal way to get into the position so that your skis will remain in the correct V-shape and
10 skid smoothly along the slope. Supporting yourself on your sticks on the slope, ensure your skis are in a comfortable V-shape with the tips about 10 centimetres apart. It is inadvisable to bring your knees too close together. Should you do so, the ski tips may cross and
15 foul your manoeuvre. Then stand perpendicular to the slope with your legs straight and stiff. Kneel towards the tips of your skis. This 'sets' the edges correctly. Without moving knees and feet, relax at the hips and sag downwards. Be careful not to slump backwards,
20 as the skis may run away with you and the tips may move apart. You should always try to avoid skiing out of control, as you are then a danger to others.

You should now be in perfect balance and should be able to lift your sticks. From a gentle push with them,
25 you should begin to slide effortlessly down the slope.

c Read the following statements and then read through the text again and decide which of the statements are true (T) or false (F). Put don't know (?) if the text doesn't tell you.
1 All beginners must learn how to snowplough.
2 Advanced skiers never use short skis.
3 Your skis must be parallel when in the snowplough position.
4 To stop or slow down, you should lean backwards.
5 The sticks are useful to you when learning to snowplough.

Vocabulary

d Look at the text and work out the meaning of the following.
1 to manœuvre
2 to foul
3 to set the edges of the skis
4 to sag
5 to slump

e Look at the following words which might be used when instructing someone in a sport. Can you match them up to form opposites?

to relax   stiff
tense   bent
to panic   to be nervous
supple   to be calm
straight   relaxed

How would you use them when instructing a tense beginner skier?

2 Grammar Modal auxiliary *should*

a Each of the following sentences contains a different use of the modal *should*. Match the uses given below with the correct sentence.

Uses:
a) advice   c) prediction or assumption
b) condition   d) obligation

1 *You should do as instructed.*
2 *They should be home by now.*
3 *Should you see him, let me know.*
4 *I should see a doctor if I were you.*

Look through the text in **1b** and underline each occurrence of *should*. Match each with the uses (a–d) above.

b Rewrite the following sentences using *should* and state the use it illustrates.
For example:
Why don't you start with some warm-up exercises?
► *You **should** start with some warm-up exercises.* (advice)

1 If you fall when cold and stiff, you may hurt yourself.
2 After a few lessons you'll feel more confident.
3 Keep out of the way of faster skiers.
4 It's a good idea to watch out for rocks.
5 By the end of your first day you'll feel exhausted.
6 Buy your own equipment, provided you seriously intend to learn.
7 Mind you get a good pair of waterproof trousers.
8 Make sure you read the local regulations.

c Now think of a sport with which you are familiar. Write 10 sentences containing *should* addressed to someone learning the sport. Try to include the different uses of *should*.

d In pairs, one student (the instructor) should try to explain how to (and how **not** to) snowplough from the picture in **1a** using the grammar and vocabulary from this unit. The other student (the skier) should obey the instructions. Then compare the skier's position with the picture and what it says in the text in **1b**.

3 Listening

🔲 **a**   Listen to the first part of the tape and find out the following.

      1   Who is speaking?
      2   Who is listening?
      3   What is the purpose of this talk?
      4   What are they going to do afterwards?

🔲 **b**   Now listen to the complete extract and tick (√) which of the following expressions are used. What is their function?

      1   Whatever you do,   5   It's no good (-ing) . . .
         don't . . .   6   Be careful not to . . .
      2   Watch out (for) . . .   7   Ensure . . .
      3   It is inadvisable . . .   8   Mind you (don't) . . .
      4   It's pointless . . .   9   Make sure . . .

      Which of the above would you be more likely to use in formal English (F) and which in informal English (I)? Which phrases seem to be neutral (N)?

   c   Look at these two sets of notes taken from the ski instructor's talk. One was written by the good pupil and the other by the not-so-good pupil. Which is which?

NOTES A

fall down : skis downhill
out of control • deep snow,
get off piste.
lost ski : Shout 'piste'
fall on lift • let go, get out of
the way.
bindings?
watch out for ice

NOTES B

fall over get up quickly
• out of the way
• keep piste clear
• skis
change direction or stop
• mind other skiers
• look behind
'piste'
• someone wants to pass
'ski'
• lost ski
drag lift
• fall - let go
• out of the way
• check

Note-taking

 d   But even the good pupil missed a few points! So listen again. In pairs, take notes yourselves and exchange the information to make sure you have everything the instructor mentioned.

4 Writing

It might have been useful for the instructor to give her pupils a written set of instructions to take away with them. From your notes and using the grammar and vocabulary you have practised, write the instructions for a beginners' ski class.

Extension eight

a Fill in the blanks in the text below with one suitable word.

Falling down is one of the hazards . . . . (1) skiing, and even . . . . (2) can be taught. Some experts . . . . (3) the ski world believe that . . . . (4) beginners to fall is wrong, because it is defensive. . . . . (5) may well be right, ... (6) there are always pupils who get . . . . (7) into trouble, so it is better to learn how to fall . . . . (8). It is best to fall backwards and sideways into the hill if you . . . . (9) your balance and cannot avoid . . . . (10). As you go down, clench your ski sticks tightly and straighten your legs to . . . . (11) that your knees do . . . . (12) dig into the slope. If they . . . . (13), you could hurt yourself. . . . . (14) sit down on the backs of your skis: . . . . (15) is a recipe for disaster. You would probably gather speed, go . . . . (16) of control, and endanger other . . . . (17) users, as well as . . . . (18). Falling is . . . . (19) to be embarrassed about; all the world's great skiers do . . . . (20) at some time.

b Match the words in A with the appropriate definition in B (the first is done as an example for you).

A		B	
1	solecism **k)**	a)	appear, develop
2	neologism	b)	basic, essential
3	semantics	c)	new word or expression
4	incongruous	d)	the study of meaning
5	transmission	e)	not natural, made by man
6	compel	f)	exact copy
7	orthodox	g)	upright, at an angle of 90°
8	establish	h)	sending (a message)
9	spur	i)	force
10	concept	j)	hold back, hinder, restrain
11	utterance	k)	breaking the rules of language
12	confidential	l)	something expected, hoped for
13	oration	m)	formal speech made on a public occasion
14	prospect	n)	secret
15	inhibit	o)	generally accepted (ideas)
16	perpendicular	p)	something said
17	replica	q)	idea
18	artificial	r)	set up, create, form
19	fundamental	s)	a motive for doing something
20	emerge	t)	not in harmony, out of place

c   Complete the following table wherever possible.
    Use a prefix in the last column.

Noun	Verb	Adjective	Opposites
1 equality	equalize	equal	inequality, unequal
2	....	appropriate	....
3	inform	....	....
4 person	....	....	....
5	....	logical	....
6	interest	....	....
7 prediction	....	....	....
8	compliment	....	....
9 efficiency	....	....	....
10	....	natural	....
11	manifest	....	....
12 accuracy	....	....	....
13	....	perfect	....
14	familiarize	....	....
15 approval	....	....	....
16	convene	....	....
17	....	comfortable	....
18 confidence	....	....	....
19	instruct	....	....
20	....	correct	....

d   Rewrite the following, beginning with the words given. Make any
    changes necessary.

1   You can always improve your English by doing a lot of reading.
    One way ...
2   How about finding a magazine on a subject that interests you?
    I should ...
3   There's no need to read every single page.
    It's no good ...
4   It is also important not to have to use your dictionary too often.
    You shouldn't ...
5   In order to achieve this, read the whole article once without stopping.
    Try ...
6   This will then give you some idea of what the article is all about.
    This way you ...
7   Don't worry about the unknown words.
    It is pointless ...
8   If you try to understand every single word, you will probably fail.
    Should ...
9   You should guess the meaning of many of these words.
    It's a good idea ...
10 To do this, read the article again, paragraph by paragraph.
    One way ...

9
On the move

1 Reading / Listening

Prediction

a How much do you know about the migration of animals?
In groups, discuss the following questions.

1 Why do animals migrate?
2 How do they know when to migrate?
3 How do they know where to go?
4 How do they know how to get there?

Which of these questions do you find most difficult to answer?
Which question do you think scientists find most difficult?

Gist reading

b Read the following text for the answer to the previous question.

It is perhaps easy enough to identify good ecological reasons why animals should migrate, and even to appreciate that the timing of migrations might be determined by environmental cues such as changing day-length or temperature. The real mystery that has baffled scientist and non-scientist alike over the centuries has been how the migrants know which way to go. To arrive at a pinpoint in the middle of an uncharted ocean is no mean feat for human navigators, even with modern satellite navigation systems to hand. That 'mere' animals can achieve the same without the advantage of even the crudest sextant or compass seems little short of miraculous.

Pronunciation

c Look carefully at the meaning of the first sentence in the text above and decide which words are emphasized more than others. Underline these words, then read the sentence aloud.

1 Do you think the words you underlined contain new information?
2 Do they contrast with other words?
3 Are the words nouns, verbs, adjectives, adverbs or . . .?

Now underline the words you think should be stressed in the rest of the text, then read it aloud. Does it sound correct?

d Listen to a recording of the text and compare the stress with your answers to the previous exercise.

2 Reading / Speaking

a Read the following extracts and plot the route taken by the shearwater, eel and cuckoo on the map given opposite.

1 The great shearwater spends the winter in the coastal areas of the North Atlantic and breeds in the South Atlantic, where the isolated volcanic island of Tristan da Cunha, a mere dot in the middle of nowhere, provides the site for some of its main colonies.

2 The European eel spawns in the Sargasso Sea, midway between the Caribbean and the bulge of West Africa. The eggs develop into larvae that drift with the currents across the European continental shelf where they become elvers and swim up the estuaries and rivers to grow into adults. Once fully grown, the adult finds its way back to the spawning grounds off the Sargasso Sea.

3 The New Zealand bronze cuckoo hatches in the nest of a non-migratory species in New Zealand. It then flies 3,000 kilometres northwest across the sea to the species wintering grounds on the Melanesian archipelago.

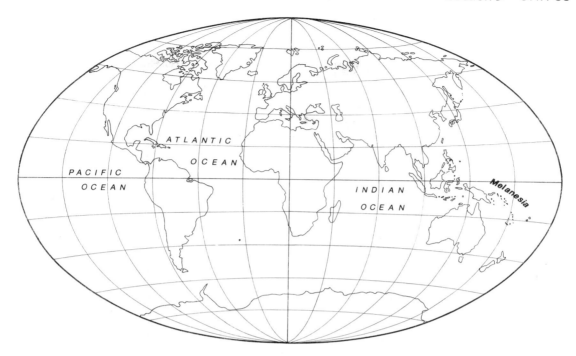

b Discuss which of the three journeys is most remarkable from the point of view of a) distance, b) accuracy.

3 Reading

Locating specific information

a 1 In the text that follows say which living creatures are mentioned in:
Paragraph 1 ....
Paragraph 2 ....
Paragraph 3 ....
Paragraph 4 ....
Paragraph 5 ....

2 How do they know which way to go? The explanations mentioned in the text are:
Paragraph 1 ...*None*...
Paragraph 2 ....
Paragraph 3 ....
Paragraph 4 ....
Paragraph 5 ....

3 Which of the explanations given above does the writer find convincing? Do you agree?

4 Which of the theories mentioned in the text are based on experimentation?

As early as the 1950s, Gustav Kramer at the Max Planck Institute at Wilhelmshaven recognized that homing in pigeons involved two distinct stages. The first covered the route from the point of release back to the general vicinity of the home loft; the second involved the simpler task of relocating the loft once the bird was back on familiar territory.

How do pigeons manage to negotiate stage one? Various theories have been put forward over the years, ranging from the mystical (telepathy) to the unlikely (infra-red detection). The earliest experimental evidence came in 1950, when Kramer and the Nobel laureate, Karl von Frisch independently published proof that starlings and honeybees, respectively, use the sun in navigation. The significant point about these results was that they implied that the animals were able to compensate for the sun's movement across the sky. Because of this movement, a route taken at a fixed angle to the sun results in a U-shaped path. In order to use the sun as a compass, it is necessary to determine a fixed reference point (such as its position at midday or the point on the horizon where it rises or sets). Since then, a vast range of species from insects to rodents have been shown to use the sun as a compass.

But many migrant birds fly only at night and so cannot use the sun as a compass. Humans have learned to navigate very competently at night using the stars, in particular the 'fixed' stars that lie on the earth's axis of rotation and therefore always appear in the same place night after night. In the late 1950s, Franz Sauer and his wife were able to show that migrating warblers could orient correctly under an artificial sky in a planetarium. These findings generated two decades of experimental work using planetaria to explore the star compasses of the nocturnal migrants. Perhaps the most intriguing aspect of this was the finding of Steven Emlen of Cornell University that, contrary to the Sauers' original supposition, the use of the stars for navigation is not innate but has to be learned. His experiments with young indigo buntings showed, not only that the star patterns have to be learned through exposure to the skies at an early stage in life, but individual birds may learn to fixate on different reference stars in the small cluster of constellations that lie over the pole.

The idea that animals might use the earth's magnetic field to orient themselves was first suggested almost a century ago, but it received little serious attention until the 1960s when an extensive series of experiments were carried out on warblers by F. W. Merkel and his associates at the University of Frankfurt (notably in more recent years, Wolfgang Wiltschko). This astounding claim led to a good deal of experimentation, as a result of which species as diverse as bees, moths, amphibians, fish, birds, mice and people have been shown to be capable of using the earth's magnetic field to orient correctly.

In his encyclopaedic review *The Evolutionary Ecology of Animal Migration*, Robin Baker of Manchester University has suggested that almost all long-distance migrations can be accounted for by piloting. He argues that, as a result of both migration flights and local exploratory movements, an animal has a rough idea of the lie of the land over an area far beyond the normal limits of its home range. There is something to be said for this view, for birds flying at an altitude of, say, 1,500 metres can see a horizon that is 80 km away, while prominent landmarks such as mountain peaks would be visible from very much further away.

Vocabulary

b Complete the following table wherever possible.

Noun(s)	Verb	Adjectives
1	....	migratory, migrant
2 exploration / explorer	....	....
3	navigate	....
4	rotate	....
5 location	....	....
6	detect	....
7 ecology	....	....
8	....	environmental
9	experiment	....
10	negotiate	....
11	....	compensatory
12	suppose	....
13	....	diverse
14 evolution	....	....

In pairs, compare your answers and check them with a dictionary.

c Underline the 'odd one out' in the following (refer to the text in **3a** opposite if necessary). Give reasons for your answers.

1 remarkable crude miraculous astounding amazing
2 result in lead to generate identify cause
3 star constellation starling planetarium
4 insect warbler rodent amphibian bird
5 navigation compass task axis pole
6 altitude flight horizon proof pilot

4 Writing

Summarizing

a Use the information from the text in **3a** to make notes on the questions below. Use your notes to write a summary of the text in not more than 400 words.

1 What was revealed by the earliest experimental evidence?
2 What was significant about this evidence?
3 What were the Sauers' findings?
4 What was intriguing about the research that developed from their work?
5 What astounding claim was made in the 1960s?
6 What theory is being put forward by Robin Baker?

b Now give your summary a title.

1 Speaking / Listening

a   Look at the illustration, then, in pairs, discuss the following questions.
1 Where are these people?
2 How does the man behind the desk feel?
3 What do you think the man with glasses is saying?

Gist listening

 b   1 Listen to the first part of the conversation and find out what the man with glasses says.
How would you reply?
2 Now listen to the rest of the conversation and note down what each of the following countries offers the holiday-maker.

Albania   Oman   Egypt   Spain

Which holiday will the couple take?

Pronunciation

▭ c Listen and underline the word or words stressed in each of the following sentences. What kinds of words are stressed?

1 'That might be just a little difficult.'
2 'That does sound exciting.'
3 'I suppose you have got some more exciting holidays.'
4 'That would be nice.'
5 'I do like beaches.'
6 'That could be a bit different.'

▭ d Listen again and match each of the above sentences to one of the thought balloons below to show what each speaker really means or might be thinking.

(a) *I'm not **completely** convinced.*

(b) *It's going to be **extremely** difficult.*

(c) *It sounds incredibly boring.*

(d) *. . . or is that too much to expect?*

(e)

(f) *Not again!*

2 Grammar   Generic reference

a Look at how we talk about things in general, for example one type of animal:

a) *The killer whale is a dangerous mammal.*
b) *A killer whale is a dangerous mammal.*
c) *Killer whales are dangerous mammals.*

Killer whale is a countable noun. If we want to talk in general about an uncountable noun, for example *wine*, *literature* or *music*, there is only one possibility:

d) *Wine is a very popular drink in Europe.*

Look at the following nouns and decide if they are countable or uncountable. Then, using the patterns a–d, make a general statement about each.

1 beer	6 cafe	11 tourist
2 beach	7 art	12 shopping
3 leather	8 village	13 souvenir
4 castle	9 sport	14 hospitality
5 sunshine	10 holiday	15 sightseeing

b Sometimes we want to make limited general reference. For example, we do not want to talk about all music, only that in Spain:

I'm very fond of $\left\{ \begin{array}{l} \textit{the music of Spain.} \\ \textit{(the) music from Spain.} \\ \textit{Spanish music.} \end{array} \right.$

Music, of course, is an uncountable noun, but the rules are the same for a countable noun, which is placed in the plural:

She much prefers $\left\{ \begin{array}{l} \textit{the souvenirs of Spain.} \\ \textit{(the) souvenirs from Spain.} \\ \textit{Spanish souvenirs.} \end{array} \right.$

c Practise making general statements and limited general statements.

First make a general statement, for example:
Ancient buildings are always interesting to visit.

Then limit the statement by referring to your own country, for example:
And the ancient buildings of France are especially popular with tourists.

Use the nouns in **2a** or any others of your choice.

3 Reading

Jigsaw reading

a In pairs, one of you read text **C** on p.197 and the other, text **D** on p.198. Discuss which country you think it is. Then tell your partner why it would be good to visit this country.

b In pairs, match these headlines with the advertisements.
1 'You'll bring home more than a sun-tan'
2 'Wake up to a view that delighted a king 500 years ago'

Why do you think both advertisements make a connection between their last two lines and their headline?

c Which of the following best summarizes what each of the advertisements is trying to tell us about this country?
1 One country – a thousand holidays
2 Everything under the sun
3 You may think you know us
4 Ancient and modern side by side

Vocabulary

d Find four phrases in the texts that refer to value.

1 ....

2 ....

3 ....

4 ....

e Find the 'odd one out' in each of these groups of adjectives.

1 historic   age-old   elderly   ancient
2 majestic   monastic   regal   royal
3 popular   secluded   deserted   isolated

f Many adjectives formed from the names of countries have similar endings.

1 Write the adjective for each of the countries below in the column appropriate to its ending. Be careful – the form of the noun may have to be changed.
2 Fill in the final column to show how you refer to a person from each of the countries.
3 Add any other countries you can think of.

a) China
b) Israel
c) Greece
d) Burma
e) Sweden
f) Thailand
g) Portugal
h) Italy
i) Turkey
j) Japan
k) Venezuela
l) England
m) Brazil
n) Ireland
o) Switzerland
p) France
q) Wales
r) Scotland
s) Pakistan
t) Denmark

Country	Nationality adjective					Person
	-ish	-ese	-(ia)n	-i	(other)	a/an
Spain	Spanish					a Spaniard

g Using the vocabulary in the table above make statements about each country, either serious, or funny.
Begin with your own country!
Examples:
The English are famous for their command of foreign languages.
English vegetables are well known for their tastelessness.

4 Writing

Pre-writing

a Put these sentences in the correct order to form an advertisement (the first one is done for you). Then place the correct article in the gaps: *a*, *the*, or *x* (to indicate that no article is necessary).

WHERE ARE ALL THE TOURISTS?

a) There are countless deserted coves along our coasts. Go and discover one and make it your own.

b) Leave your car outside . . . . high white village walls.

c) We could tell you of peaceful places all around Spain, but you'll have more fun finding them for yourself.

d) Up the mountainside, just a short drive from some of our best-known beach resorts are . . . . ancient villages sleeping alone and still as lizards in . . . . sunshine.

e) Then they will become . . . . places you will always remember most fondly, where there wasn't . . . . tourist in sight.

f) They're five minutes' drive from here, at one of . . . . busiest, most popular beaches in Spain. ①

g) Except you. There's peace and quiet inland, too.

h) The streets will be too narrow for it, and sometimes they become . . . . steps. There will be . . . . church and . . . . small square. There will be . . . . tables outside . . . . café.

i) One reason why so many people come to Spain, and come back year after year, is that we have so many secluded spots like this beach.

j) Sit, sip some wine and listen to . . . . quiet.

Free writing

b   Imagine you went on a holiday which turned out to be very different from the way it was presented in the three advertisements in this unit. Write a letter describing the holiday to a friend. You can make use of the grammar and vocabulary you have practised, like this:
They said Spanish leather was very cheap but the leather in Barcelona was quite expensive.
You should not of course use this pattern too often!

UNIT 35 EXPLORATIONS

1 Speaking   In pairs or groups, discuss the following questions.

1 Where do you think the photograph below was taken?
2 What kind of boat is it?
3 Why do you think it was built?

2 Listening   Listen to the first part of an interview, then answer the following questions.

1 What is the name of the boat pictured above?
2 What kind of boat is it?
3 Who sailed in the original boat?
4 In what period was the original built?
5 How long did it take to build the boat pictured above?

3 Reading

a   Read the text opposite and complete the following information.

1 Size of ship: ....
2 Made of: ....
3 Number of oars: ....
4 Where it was built: ....

A sleek galley, its twenty long oars darting as one into the blue waves of the Aegean glides swiftly out of the old harbour on the island of Spetses; a man dressed in a red wind-cheater stands at the helm and grips the side rudder. The ship turns sleekly into the wind. As the ship powers on past the new harbour, where a blue and yellow hydrofoil nudges against the concrete landing, a shout goes up from a harbour-side table of elderly men: 'The Argo! The Argo!'

The man in red is the writer, adventurer and maritime historian, Tim Severin. The ship is the vessel for his latest project which begins this month — the retracing of the legendary route of Jason and the Argonauts in their quest for the Golden Fleece.

The beech and pine wood hull of the modern Argo, a fifty-two foot replica of a Bronze Age Greek galley, was built, virtually single-handedly, by the traditional shipwright Vassilis Delimitros on the island of Spetses where, legend has it, the original Argo was built. It took less than six months — despite experts' predictions that it would take at least three years. 'Given the back up, given the encouragement,' Severin asserts, 'people will work wonders.'

Vocabulary

b Complete the labelling of the diagram below, using words from the text.

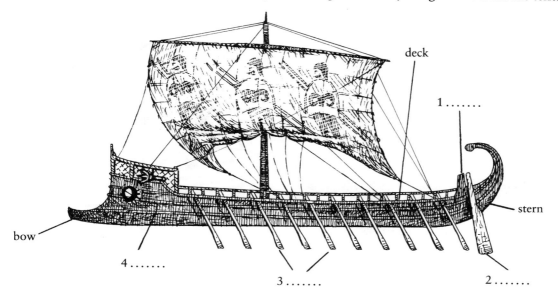

deck

1 . . . .

stern

bow

4 . . . .

3 . . . .

2 . . . .

4 Listening

Gist listening

a Listen to the rest of the interview with Tim Severin. What is his aim in recreating legendary voyages?

Locating specific information

b Listen to the second part of the interview again and draw lines to match the information about the voyages in the three columns below.

Who	From	To
Sindbad	Ireland	China
Brendan	Volos	America
Jason	Muscat	Georgia

c Listen again to both parts of the interview. Which of the following do you hear on the tape, a) or b)?

1 a) This spectacular voyage
   b) This particular voyage
2 a) What is based on fact
   b) What is based in fact
3 a) You actually reconstructed
   b) You've actually reconstructed
4 a) It must've taken
   b) It must have taken
5 a) St Brendan could've crossed
   b) St Brendan could have crossed
6 a) We're heading for Georgia
   b) We head for Georgia

The Brendan Voyage

The Sindbad Voyage

5 Reading

Locating specific information

a Read the text below and answer these questions.
1 What problems might Severin's crew face on the voyage?
2 What problems did Jason's crew face?

Severin's truly international crew is comprised of a nucleus of ten Irish, American, English and Danish sailors and includes a photographer, a navigator, a shipwright, a cook and an artist. Several members of the team have crewed for the 44-year-old writer/adventurer on previous projects – notably the seven-and-a-half-month voyage to China which was undertaken in a replica Arab dhow – and the famous Brendan Voyage in a replica leather 'currach' which St Brendan is believed to have used in an Atlantic crossing from Ireland to North America in the 6th century BC, nine hundred years before Columbus.

The remaining fifty per cent of the crew will alternate, with Greeks participating in Greek waters, Turks in Turkish waters and Soviet citizens in Soviet waters.

'We're going to have to learn to live with each other,' Severin observes. 'I mean, there'll be twenty men together in a very small boat. People used to be accustomed to living in close, confined quarters 3,000 years ago. We're going to have to learn to do it again.'

The voyage is expected to last three and a half months. After leaving Volos, the original point of departure, the crew will row and sail through the Dardanelles into the Sea of Marmara and then across the northern Turkish Black Sea coast to Soviet Georgia – the ancient land of Colchis.

'It's a coasting voyage,' Severin notes. 'In the Bronze Age, they didn't like to be out of sight of land. This sort of boat is not designed for sea passages of any length. In any case you can't sleep twenty on board.

You've got to go ashore at night to get some rest. It makes it much more interesting for me from the historical side and as a geographer – trying to identify where stops were made on that voyage.'

Severin, who has written many popular books on the history of exploration, believes that voyaging up through the Bosporus is going to be a major problem. 'There's a very strong south-going current sometimes. We need to have a good day when the current is slack. Ideally, we need a slight southerly wind to help us. But that's why we have to start early in the season – because that's our only chance for southerly winds.' In fact, according to Severin, this kind of trip only ever occurred during the summer months. 'The absolute lesson I've learned on two previous voyages,' he says, 'is that you never break out of the traditional sailing season. In Jason's time, they just spent the winter at home.'

One hopes that Severin and his Argonauts will be made more welcome than Jason and his crew – who at various times had to deal with clashing rocks, hordes of Harpies, aggressive Amazons, wild, fire-breathing oxen and a particularly nasty army of warriors which sprang up from the ground wherever their 'seeds' – dragon's teeth – had been scattered. Of course, Jason had several influential goddesses on his side. He lacked, however, the modern safety equipment on whose aid Severin will be relying in times of crisis.

Vocabulary

b Which two words are names of types of boat?
a) .... b) ....

c Which is the 'odd one out' in the following lists? Give reasons for your answer.
1 voyage travel journey trip
2 shipwright historian navigator sailor
3 hull rudder helm wind-cheater stern
4 row sail quest glide
5 leather replica pine beech bronze

d Read the text again and complete the following diagram.

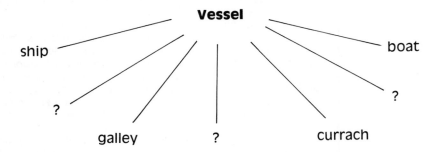

e Tick (√) those of the following words which mean 'to do something again'.

1 re-create ☐
2 reconstruct ☐
3 retrace ☐
4 recount ☐
5 recapture ☐
6 reproduce ☐
7 research ☐
8 rely ☐
9 reprove ☐
10 re-learn ☐
11 re-enact ☐
12 rewrite ☐

Say each word out loud and underline the syllable that you stress. Do you notice any patterns?

6 Grammar Modal auxiliaries

Modal perfects

a In the interview you heard:

It must have taken some time to build.
St Brendan could have crossed from the Kerry Coast to the New World.

Which sentence expresses the greatest degree of certainty?
In which sentence could you use *might have* or *may have* to express a similar meaning?

Below each of the following sentences are some notes. Complete these to make a second sentence using *must have* or *could have* as appropriate.
Example:
The replica Argo cost a lot to build.
Severin/have/financial help
▶ *Severin must have had financial help.*

1 The crew of the original Argo consisted of twenty men.
  It / be crowded/on board
2 It is possible that Jason sailed the route Severin is taking.
  Jason / take / same route / Severin
3 Severin is sure the original voyage took place in summer – the only time when currents and winds are right.
  Severin / believe/original / voyage / take place / summer
4 Severin wants to identify the probable stages of the original voyage.
  Severin / try / find / places / original Argo / stop
5 Severin's vessel was built on Spetses; according to legend this is where the original was built.
  It be thought / original Argo / be built on Spetses
6 Severin is sure that Sindbad couldn't have been one person.
  Severin / believe / character of Sindbad / be made up / from several historical figures

Short answers using modals

b Look at the following to see how we give a short answer with these modal constructions:

Could she have missed the train? Yes, she could (have).
Might he have been playing football? Yes, he might have been.
Will he be sitting at home? No, he won't (be).

Use a modal to form questions from the following notes. Then take it in turns to ask questions and give short answers. Think about the tense of the questions and base your answers on what you have learnt about Severin so far.
Example:
Tim/plan/voyage/for a long time?
▶ *Could Tim have been planning the voyage for a long time?*
▶ *Yes, he must have been.*
1 Tim / regret / decision / sail the Argo?
2 original Argo / be built / Spetses?
3 it / cost / as much as / new model?
4 new model / be stronger / old one?
5 such a boat / sail / far from land?
6 Tim / have difficulties / find / crew?
7 Tim / have financial help / for voyage?
8 Tim/be one of most adventurous writers?

7 Writing

Pre-writing

a Fill in the gaps in the text below using the sentences in the box.

> a) Severin believes Sindbad to have been a fictional composite of historical Arab sea captains who ventured to the very edge of the world as they knew it.
>
> b) The best-selling book *Brendan Voyage* describes a hair-raising expedition in which Severin proves that St Brendan, a 6th-century Irish abbot, could have crossed from the Kerry Coast to the New World in a boat made locally from ox-hides.
>
> c) He actually lives the part of the legendary figures he writes about.
>
> d) The danger of capsize was always present.
>
> e) In those days, however, they lacked the modern safety equipment on whose aid Severin relies in times of crisis.

1 Tim Severin describes himself as primarily a writer of books which bring legends to life. ....
....

2 In order to reconstruct his boat Severin studied and reproduced medieval materials and technology. ....
....

3 On board the 'Brendan', the race was on against gales, storms and fogs.
....
It never happened.

4 Conditions were not very different in the Indian Ocean during the equally famous Sindbad voyage. ....
That was to the 8th century what space exploration is to the 20th.

5 Tim Severin is one of the most adventurous writers living today. ....
....
Doing everything the way they would have done it.

Free writing

b Find out about any other famous explorer, living or dead, and write about his or her life and achievements.

UNIT 36 SURVIVAL

1 Speaking

a *'Sailing is the most expensive way to travel slowly and uncomfortably.'*
In pairs, discuss:
   1 Have you ever sailed? What was it like?
   2 Would you agree with the statement above?
   3 Can you think of more uncomfortable ways to travel?

b A man once sold his farm and animals, everything he had, to buy an old
sailing boat and take his family on an educational cruise round the world.
In pairs, discuss:
   1 What do you think of this idea?
   2 Which countries would you visit and why?
   3 If you were a young child, would you like to go?
       As a parent, would you do this?
   4 Think of all the things that might go wrong.

2 Reading

Gist reading

a Now read this text once quickly and find out what did go wrong.

With my sextant carefully replaced in its box I had turned to my books
to work up a reasonably accurate dead-reckoning position when
sledgehammer blows of incredible force struck the hull beneath my feet
hurling me against the bunk, the noise of the impact almost deafening
my ears to the roar of inrushing water. I heard Lyn call out, and almost
at the same time heard the cry of 'Whales!' from the cockpit. My senses
still reeled as I dropped to my knees and tore up the floorboards to gaze
in horror at the blue Pacific through the large splintered hole punched
up through the hull planking between two of the grown oak frames.
Water was pouring up through the hole with torrential force and although
Lyn called out that it was no use, that the water was pouring in from
another hole under the WC flooring as well, I jammed my foot on the
broken strakes and shouted to her to give me large cloths, anything to
stem the flood. She threw me a pillow and I jammed it down on top
of the broken planking, rammed the floorboard on top and stood on
it; the roar of the incoming water scarcely diminished, it was already
above the level of the floorboards as I heard Douglas cry from the deck
'Are we sinking, Dad?' 'Yes! Abandon ship!'; my voice felt remote
as numbly I watched the water rise rapidly up the engine casing; it was
lapping my knees as I turned to follow Lyn, already urging Neil and
Robin on deck.

Locating specific information

b Read the text again and complete this summary.

The whales hit the boat with such force that I was .... (1).
I knew what had caused the impact because .... (2).
I tried to find where the water was coming in by .... (3).
Although Lyn told me that .... (4), I tried
to stop the water by .... (5). But we were
sinking, so I told everybody .... (6).

c Decide whether the following are true (T) or false (F). Put (?) for 'don't know'.

1 The noise of the whales hitting the boat was louder than the sound of the water rushing in.
2 It was Lyn who saw the whales.
3 The story is told by the father.
4 The boat was hit by more than one whale.
5 The man had no idea what to do when he saw the hole.
6 The boat began to sink very quickly.

Vocabulary

d Find the words in the text that mean the following.

1 a built-in bed
2 the place from where the boat is steered
3 an instrument used for finding a boat's position
4 the body of a boat
5 long, flat pieces of wood
6 the platform which provides a floor for those outside and a ceiling for those inside the boat

e 1 In the text, which of these words refer to violent action and which to water? Put a tick (√) in the appropriate box.

	Violent action	Water
sledgehammer	☐	☐
strike	☐	☐
roar	☐	☐
impact	☐	☐
tear up	☐	☐
pour	☐	☐
torrential	☐	☐
jam	☐	☐
hurl	☐	☐
stem	☐	☐
lap	☐	☐
ram	☐	☐

2 Can you explain the difference between *blow* and *force* as in *sledgehammer blow*, *incredible force*, *torrential force*?

3 The following are all verbs which can refer to the action of water. Which is the 'odd one out' and why?

roar   pour   rush   flood   lap

Text-attack skills

f Look through the text and find the two most common ways in which the author links two actions taking place **at the same time**. What other ways can you think of?

3 Speaking / Listening

Discussion

a In groups of three, discuss the following situation and the questions which follow over the page.

The boat in which you and your family are sailing around the world has sunk. You are now in a small sailing boat (1.3 metres long) in the Pacific Ocean. Land lies 4,500 km to the west and 2,000 km to the north-east. There is a small group of islands 300 km to the south-east. The wind and currents travel in a north-easterly direction. You are 500 km from the nearest shipping lanes.

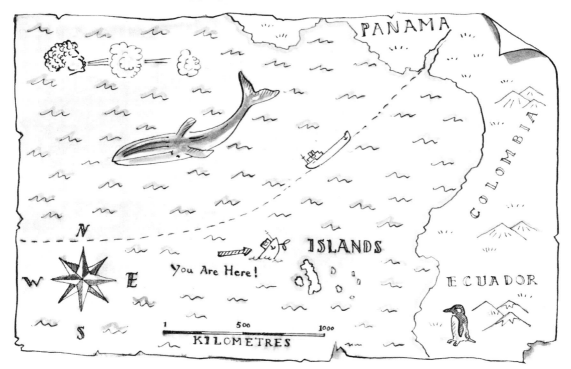

1 Would you
  a) stay where you are and wait for rescue?
  b) row against the wind and currents to the islands to the east?
  c) sail to land in the west?
  d) sail to land in the north-east?
2 Which would you fear the most?
  a) thirst b) sharks c) heat d) storms e) boredom
3 What could you drink?
4 What would you talk about?
5 What could you eat?
6 How could you pass the time?

Gist listening

 b Listen and find out the following information.
1 Who is speaking?
2 Where are they?
3 What is happening?

Note-taking

 c Listen again in groups of three. Look at questions 1–6 in **3a** above and each take notes on how the family answers the questions. How do their answers compare with yours?
Then exchange your information with the others in your group.

4 Writing

Imagine what happened to the Robertson family happened to you, and you have just been rescued. Using the vocabulary and the information from this unit write a letter to your best friend telling him/her
1 how your boat sank.
2 how you survived.
3 how you were rescued.

Remember to use some of the ways of linking two actions you looked at in **2f**.

Extension nine

a Fill each of the blanks in the sentences below by choosing a suitable form of one of the following words.

ancient	rely	compass	compensate
explore	baffle	experiment	research
retrace	impact	navigation	negotiate
miraculous	replica	tear up	hair-raising
voyage	torrential	migrate	hurl

The boat looked like a . . . . (1) of a Roman galley. And it was powered only by an . . . . (2) engine, leaking oil. What sails I could see resembled . . . . (3) old shirts. The hull itself had clearly survived at least one major . . . . (4). I couldn't see any . . . . (5) instruments at all.

To . . . . (6) for all these drawbacks was the added sense of adventure. My aim was to . . . . (7) some deserted islands to the south. I had heard they lay on the . . . . (8) route of several New Zealand birds. And it was this route that I was trying to . . . . (9). I had no evidence up to this point and was . . . . (10) on local fishermen's stories. So I was hoping my little . . . . (11) would be successful. It might at least solve a problem that had . . . . (12) me. And enable me to complete an important part of my . . . . (13) for the university.

Having . . . . (14) a suitable sum for the hire of the boat and crew, we set off. Shortly afterwards we were soaked by a . . . . (15) downpour. The wind and waves rose by the minute and I was . . . . (16) from one side of the boat to the other. I began to think it was foolish of me ever to have dreamed of such a . . . . (17).

Night fell and our voyage became even more . . . . (18). In the darkness we steered with the aid of a small, crude . . . . (19). It was indeed a . . . . (20) sight to see the islands just ahead of us as the sun rose.

b Do you recognize the words below? They are all from unit 36 but the letters have been rearranged. Write them out correctly and state whether they are nouns (N), verbs (V) or adjectives (adj.) as used in unit 36.

1 mar	5 storichi	9 traceer	13 latisoed
2 lyer	6 arro	10 logycoe	14 velove
3 grateim	7 maj	11 ageyov	15 lotace
4 sediver	8 roup	12 ullh	

Can any of these words be used as any other part of speech?
If so, is there a change of meaning, for example from verb to noun?

c Make three statements for each of the following (1–5) by joining the words on the left (a–c) with one of the three completions on the right.

1 a) The shark   — are dangerous but not all.
   b) Some sharks   — with the blue tail is very
   c) Sharks   dangerous.
                          — are a frightening sight.

2 a) The music   – can be very relaxing.
   b) Music   – is far too loud – turn it down.
   c) Some music   – cannot really be called music.

3 a) He must have travelled   – but I doubt it.
     this far,   – by now.
   b) He could have travelled   – without a doubt.
     this far,
   c) He might have travelled
     this far,

4 a) The birds flew away   – while I was looking out of the
   b) The birds had built their   window.
     nests   – immediately I approached.
   c) The birds landed   – when the weather suddenly
                                    changed.

d   Fill each of the numbered blanks with one suitable word.

Migration is immense in its manifestations, highly complicated . . . . (1)
its performance, and yet on the whole remarkably regular in its annual
repetition: such a phenomenon obviously . . . . (2) problems of great
biological interest. First, a form of behaviour so expensive in energy and
so hazardous to life must serve a useful . . . . (3), i.e. have a 'survival
value' for the species, or it would not . . . . (4). Secondly, there is the
question . . . . (5) causation; merely saying that migration is useful does
. . . . (6) explain its happening, nor can it be imagined as a rational
course of action. . . . . (7), there is the question of method: how is
. . . . (8) accomplished?

Migration enables birds to exploit opportunities that would . . . . (9)
not be available. The breeding . . . . (10) provides the conditions best
suited to the . . . . (11) of the species: appropriate nesting sites and an
abundant food . . . . (12) at the time when it is most needed, and in
higher latitudes, long days in which to collect food for the . . . . (13).
Yet at other times of the year the area may be incapable of . . . . (14)
even non-reproductive life: availability of a suitable . . . . (15) is
probably more important than the direct effects of climatic conditions.
The fact that birds breed at a . . . . (16) time of year is itself evidence of
an adaptation to the . . . . (17) availability of a maximum (or
qualitatively optimum) supply of food while the young have to
. . . . (18) fed; and migration is clearly . . . . (19) to this. The whole
annual . . . . (20) of a bird's life can be seen as an alternation between
reproductive and non-reproductive states.

Jigsaw reading

Text A

Disappointing as it may seem, it must be noted that as far as 16th century England is concerned, there is no evidence to suggest the existence of anything like an organized cult with covens, black sabbaths, midnight orgies and aerial transportation (a broomstick is mentioned only once in English witchcraft trials). What we do find are lonely old women living on the edge of poverty, often reduced to begging from their neighbours who looked on them with suspicion and resentment and whose guilty conscience probably troubled them a good deal. The fact that they were women is only to be expected because old women and childless widows were economically and socially the most vulnerable members of a small rural community. Often their only companions were a pet cat, a toad or a weasel. Sometimes they kept them in a pot of wood and called them affectionate names, Grizzell or Pyewacket or Sack-and-Sugar. These were transformed in the imagination of their accusers into their 'familiars' lent them by the devil to do his evil business. If, in addition, the lonely old woman had any distinguishing marks, a hump back or hair on her chin or a 'devil's teat' under her armpit, suspicion became near certainty.

Text C

Some things never change. The morning sun lights up your bedroom in the castle, as it has done since 1600.

You could lose yourself in a daydream of timeless time, but the scent of coffee reminds you that the time is now.

The castle is now a hotel, one of hundreds like it, where you can stay in regal comfort for no more than the price of an ordinary hotel.

If you like to relive the past in your travels, you can do it all over . . . . . . Not only can you sleep in castles and palaces that have been converted to hotels, but also in historic lodgings that were built as hotels and inns.

All will offer you modern conveniences and comforts, plus the age-old tradition of . . . . . . hospitality and courtesy that does not merely answer your needs, but anticipates them. Some of the castle and palace hotels are tourist hotels run by the . . . . . . Government. Others are privately owned, often by the same family for generations. All of them will let you sleep like a king or at least a nobleman. You might call it a good knight's rest.

Text B

Witches are people supposed to be doing the work of the devil. The name 'witch' was used to describe both sexes, though witches were usually women. [5] They commonly had 'familiars' in the form of spirits disguised as animals of bad or sinister reputation — toads or cats of certain colours. To work their [10] magic, witches uttered spells of specially-devised words or they used objects ('charms') supposed to have magical properties; witches used to gather [15] in small communities known as 'covens', and they assembled on one day of the year (a 'witches' sabbath') to worship the devil. That witchcraft was common in [20] the Middle Ages is not surprising; it is at first surprising that it was common in the late 16th and early 17th centuries, and that not merely the ignorant and [25] uneducated but some of the learned believed in it. The first law making witchcraft an offence punishable by death was passed in 1603 and it was not repealed until [30] 1736.

Text D

Take an empty duffel bag with you. You're going to bring home all sorts of things you hadn't planned to buy; extraordinary things you simply couldn't resist. [5]

For example, our ceramics. They vary from pieces of museum quality to simple, charming things you'll use every day. A colourful wine jug can be had for less than the cost of [10] the wine it was meant to hold. Crafts are everywhere . . . . . . at prices you'll hardly believe. Even the fabled, intricately carved metalwork of . . . . . . inlaid [15] with pure gold and silver, costs no more than mass-produced jewellery, boxes and trays in other countries.

Leave room in your duffel bag for [20] some hand-woven textiles and a bottle or two of rare sherry. Is the bag getting full? Buy another, made of supple leather. Of course you'll bring home memories, too, [25] captured in snapshots that look like photos of dreams.

You'll remember, too, that the beaches and sunshine you came to enjoy were even better than you [30] had hoped for, simply because they were here in . . . .

Because . . . . is not just a place you go to.

It's a place you bring home with [35] you.

Text E

It is probably only a layman's idea that the creative person is peculiarly gifted with a certain quality that ordinary people do not have. This conception can be dismissed by psychologists, very likely by common consent. The general psychological conviction seems to be that all individuals possess to some degree all abilities, except for the occurrence of pathologies. Creative acts can therefore be expected, no matter how feeble or how infrequent, of almost all individuals. The important consideration here is the concept of continuity. Whatever the nature of creative talent may be, those persons who are recognized as creative merely have more of what all of us have. It is this principle of continuity that makes possible the investigation of creativity in people who are not necessarily *distinguished*.

The conception that creativity is bound up with intelligence has many followers among psychologists. Creative acts are expected from those of high IQ, and not expected from those of low IQ. The term 'genius', which was developed to describe people who *distinguish* themselves because of creative productivity, has been adopted to describe the child with exceptionally high IQ. Many regard this as unfortunate, but the custom seems to have prevailed.

There is much evidence of substantial, positive correlations between IQ as measured by an intelligence test and certain creative talents, but the extent of the correlation is unknown. The work of Terman and his associates is the best source of evidence of these correlations; and yet, this evidence is not decisive. Although it was found that *distinguished* men of history generally had high estimated IQs, it is not certain that indicators in the form of creative behaviour have not entered into those estimations (Cox, 1926). It would be much more crucial to know what the same individuals would have done on intelligence tests when they were children. Terman's study of the thousand children of exceptionally high IQs who have now reached maturity does not throw much light on this theory. Among the group there is plenty of indication of superior educational attainment and of superior vocational and social adjustment. On the other hand, there seems to be as yet little promise of a Darwin, an Edison, or a Eugene O'Neill, although the members of the group have reached the age level that has come to be recognized as the 'most creative years'. The writers on that study recognize this fact and account for it on the basis of the extreme rarity of individuals of the calibre of those whom I have mentioned (Terman and Oden, 1947). It is hoped that further follow-up studies will give due attention to criteria of a more specifically creative character.

When we look into the nature of intelligence tests, we encounter many doubts concerning their coverage of creative abilities. It should be remembered that from the time of Binet to the present, the chief practical criterion used in the validation of tests of intellect has been achievement in school. For children, this has meant largely achievement in reading and arithmetic. This fact has generally determined the nature of our intelligence tests. Operationally, then, intelligence has been the ability (or complex of abilities) to master reading and arithmetic and similar subjects. These subjects are not conspicuously demanding of creative talent.

Text F

It is obvious that we cannot explain what it is that makes for outstanding ability in creative work. We do not know enough about the human personality as a complete whole to to be able to detect the factors which make for the differences between genius, outstanding performer, and ordinary 'average' ability. The judgement may be hazarded, however, that these differences, however great, are a matter of degree. There are several considerations which point in the direction of this view.

In the first place, identical discoveries and inventions have frequently been made independently and almost simultaneously by different thinkers (Leibniz and Newton with the calculus, Darwin and Wallace with the theory of evolution of species by natural selection). Even if a genius was needed to take the step, the time was ripe for it to be taken.

Again, however gifted, the outstanding man needs training and other favourable assistance in his work. Skills and techniques must be acquired and practised, and the help of other people is needed in order that the thinker should receive stimulation and direction. Darwin and Wallace both hit on their biological theory through reading an eighteenth-century treatise on economics (Malthus on 'Population'). Kant would never have thought seriously about publishing if he had not been shaken out of his 'dogmatic slumbers' by his equally great stimulator, David Hume: it was on reading Hume's *Enquiry* that Kant really became excited about certain philosophical problems.

Creative thinking is conditioned by many (humdrum) factors which influence the genius as much as the beginner. Most of us indulge in some genuine creative activity from time to time.

What *distinguishes* the great artist or thinker is his consistently high output of good work, his deeper sensitivity, his greater flexibility and adventurousness – and, of course, his superior training and 'education for life'. Yet the difference is probably one of degree. It may be that there is some factor present in the case of the outstanding performer, which is absent in the case of the average creator and which accounts for his 'leap ahead' of normal learning, perceptual stimulation, personality traits. But if there is such a factor, we have no inkling as to what it might be.

When the time comes for an empirically grounded 'psychology of personality' we may be able to provide a more satisfying account of creative thinking. Personality factors are clearly of fundamental importance not merely in helping to define the limits of an individual's ability but also the special talents he develops and the style in which he engages in his characteristic pursuits.

Text G

The composer most universally loved and revered by muscians, who as a child prodigy was shown off throughout Europe by his father (a violinist in the Archbishop of Salzburg's service) and fêted everywhere, and who later achieved many resounding successes (such as the sensational triumph of his opera 'The Marriage of Figaro' in both Vienna and Prague), was buried in an unmarked pauper's grave at the age of thirty-five. This melancholy state of affairs, which reflects on the world's ability to accommodate a genius in its midst, arose because his natural brilliance made him outspoken and impatient of compromise with the slower-witted and those of more superficial tastes, and because of his feckless way of life at a time when freelance composing without the support of a patron was unknown.

His dazzling early life – the darling of royalty, nobility and musical connoisseurs, decorated by the Pope, and with a large number of successful performances of his compositions to his credit (including his fourth and sixth operas, written at the age of fourteen and sixteen) – did not make it easy for him to settle down in provincial Salzburg, least of all under an overbearing Archbishop, unsympathetic to music. Nor, despite continued efforts, was he able to secure a permanent appointment in any of the centres which had hailed him as a visiting keyboard player, violinist and composer. His travels, of course, broadened his experience by bringing him into contact with other composers (including Haydn, his admiration for whom was warmly reciprocated) and with leading players such as those in Mannheim, which was famous for its orchestra; but his triumphs outside Salzburg (like that of the opera 'Idomeneo' at Munich, two days after his twenty-fifth birthday) irked his master, who in 1781 literally kicked him out.

His ability to think out a work, complete in every detail, in his head explains such feats as his writing in a mere fortnight his last three great symphonies (the finale of the so-called 'Jupiter' in C being a most astonishing piece of contrapuntal virtuosity); but one of his most awesome characteristics was the sheer perfection of his technique in whatever he touched.

Text H

The composer who bears this immortal name is universally acknowledged as the world's greatest musical genius. He showed perhaps unique musical precocity, beginning to compose at about the age of five. In his short life he produced a vast output, but died poor, in spite of the fact that his genius was acknowledged. He was born in Salzburg and early in his career toured the European courts as an infant prodigy, He left the service of the Archbishop of Salzburg in his twenty-sixth year to live in Vienna where his friendship with Haydn began and where his greatest works were written. He assimilated a great variety of musical influences and mastered all the musical forms of his time. His genius lies in the effortless outpouring of all forms of music, in the ever-flowing melodies, in the consistent beauty and symmetry of his compositions and in the exactness of his method. Although he composed with great ease and speed, his music has great expressive power. The purity and grace which characterize his style, and which constitute its immediate appeal, do not preclude emotional intensity and depth. His works include forty one symphonies of which the last three (all written in 1788) are especially outstanding. They are among the loveliest and greatest works in instrumental music. His last composition, written under the shadow of death, was the Requiem Mass, a work of tragic beauty. He died at the age of thirty-five in poverty.

Tapescript

UNIT 1

A So Vera, been teaching for a while now, erm, what about students then, what makes a good student, what makes a bad student?

B Well I think the first thing you'd think about would be the student who pays attention to what's going on.

A That's pretty important.

B Er, I think it's always nice when they're enthusiastic and er . . .

A Ah, yes.

B . . . Listen to you, and things, I think that, erm, a lot of people have problems with studying though, study skills, they er you know maybe don't realize that if you tell them about something new that they should write it down or they should try and use it, and er, and well that's often a problem, I think um, and I think that some students who want to try and speak the language, well that's always important, I think, er, an awful lot of them, you know, like to speak their own language when they're here.

A You mean, in the classroom.

B In the classroom, yes. I think it's always nice when they try to speak English, er, whatever else, they . . .

A What about attitude to things like vocabulary or homework, things like that?

B Yes, well you know I think, you know personally, I don't mind especially with adult classes, I'm fairly relaxed about homework, but . . . but it's always nice to get it and it's always a good sign when they do give it because then I know, well they're interested and they want to learn more. They want to see what their mistakes are. That's another thing I think, one of the most important things is learning from their mistakes. I think you know we all do it in life.

A That's true.

B Erm, you know, if they can sort of look at a piece of homework at home, see the corrections on it and try to work out where they're going wrong, it's a great help.

A Right. Well, the good student may do that but what do you think the average student actually does with that corrected bit of homework?

B Ah, well normally I think they lose it pretty quickly. That's one of the biggest problems, I think, yes.

A Right.

B Trying to keep a notebook in order you know, with the lessons and all the work they've done. That's a big problem I think.

A Some of them seem to appear without any books at all, actually.

B Well yes, some of them with no pens either, students with no pens, it always interests me that.

A That's absolutely right.

B Straight from university, arrive here, with no pens, you know, you wonder what they do at university all day.

A Well what I wanted to ask really was: you're a teacher, been teaching for some years now, erm, what would you say, how would you describe a good student or a bad student, you know sort of things they do or don't do in the classroom?

C Erm, well, a good student is usually one who's not afraid to make mistakes, I'd say.

A Uh huh.

C And he's, er, eager to experiment with every new thing that he learns, whether it be a structure or a function or a new word, erm, he immediately starts trying to use it.

A Yeah, all right.

C And he's interested in the mistakes he makes, he's not afraid to make them.

A So he's not simply interested in having it corrected and moving on?

C No, no, no. He, he plays with the language. A bad student, on the other hand, will perhaps say 'OK I've done this chapter I know this,' without trying to experiment at all, without really testing himself .

A Ahha, ahha.

C He's usually passive, he won't speak up much in the classroom. He'll very rarely ask you why this and why not something else . . .

A Just sort of accepts what you give him and doesn't do anything more with it.

C That's right and in a test he's the one person who's likely to suddenly realize that, er yes, he wasn't too sure about that after all.

A Yeah.

C And peep over at the er . . . at his neighbour's paper.

A Oh yes, an alternative learning strategy.

C Right, and he invariably decides that the other person is more likely to be right than himself. I think that's the result of, er, this sort of unwillingness to make mistakes and stick his neck out.

A Mm, right, yeah. Er, anything else?

C Er . . .

A That characterizes the good or bad learner?

C Er, mm, the bad learner is, wait a minute er, the good learner is erm, well, I think he'll do more off his own bat as well, he won't rely entirely on the teacher.

A Mmhm.

C He'll read, he'll read books.

A Mm, so work outside the classroom as well as in it.

C Yes, yeah.

A Yeah, yeah.

C Students who make most progress are first of all those who experiment and secondly those who read books.

UNIT 2

I was employed by the Modern Language Teachers' Association to go over there to talk about teaching methods, erm for the teaching of French in this case, and it was obviously a very big event – they gave me a complete, erm, suite in a really plush hotel, oh it had a front door and a back door and a bathroom and had a sitting-room and a . . . bedroom and a kitchen, I mean it was a really big deal, cost them a fortune. Three hundred people came from all over, very very expensive . . . lot of money poured into it and it, well you know, it went reasonably well – I enjoyed it anyway and then at the end of this whole thing I was taken to the airport by erm, the organizer, a woman called Yolanda Woodlands and she'd, well I thought she'd done a great, great organizational job and it had obviously gone well for her and it had gone well for me so we were sitting there, I suppose preening ourselves a little bit and she was saying to me something like, er, 'Well it sure was a great conference, Andrew.' 'Yes, yeah, good, good, I think it went all right didn't it?' 'Sure, sure I think you did just a wonderful job, just a wonderful job.' 'Oh, thank you very much Yolanda.' 'Yes of course we knew it would be just, we knew it would be a wonderful job, we knew it would be.' 'Oh, that's er . . . that's very kind of you.' 'Yes we were absolutely certain it was going to be a wonderful job, after all we, we had to be certain because you know, bringing you all this way out here and all this money we were going to put into it, it just had to be, just had to be wonderful.' 'Oh, oh that's very kind of you.' Oh, she was going on rather a lot; she said, 'Yes, we had er, we just you know we, we had your name checked out and it was so full of goddarned sevens we knew it, it couldn't be a flop.' I said 'Full of what?' She said, 'So full of sevens, you know I took it to a numerologist and he just looked at your name and indeed he looked at your address, your address and he said even he said, "Goddarn me," he said, "even the address is full of goddarn sevens".' And er, well I mean, so I was absolutely staggered by this because . . . er and when I showed astonishment she said, 'Well you know, you've got to realize,' she said 'you've got to realize we couldn't possibly bring you out here and take the risk that it wouldn't be successful, far too much money wrapped up in the whole thing, so we just had your name checked out. And it was, it was OK.' That was a great moment.

UNIT 5

I=Interviewer, T.B.=Tim Batstone.

I Tim, you've windsurfed around the United Kingdom. How long did it take?
T.B. Er . . . it took about 70 days altogether.
I And how did you survive during 70 days at sea?
T.B. Very . . . with great difficulty. Um . . . I think the, the first day I nearly, nearly died and er . . . after that it got steadily better.
I How did you nearly die?

T.B. Just from exhaustion. Er . . . it was the first time I had been on a windsurfer for 10 hours at a stretch and er . . . the old body er . . . just complained.
I How did you eat? I mean did you get off the surfboard?
T.B. Yes. I had er . . . a mother ship er . . . a large 46-foot yacht which followed me round and in the morning I'd have breakfast on the yacht and in the evening I'd have my evening meal and during the day I would just have sort of orange juice and biscuits.
I So you didn't touch dry land? You . . . you . . .
T.B. I did. Erm . . . I mean you have to when the tide turns you have to sometimes get out pretty quickly because tides move so fast and we'd take a radio fix of where I'd got to and we'd come out to the same spot the next day, so I certainly did touch, touch land, that was, that was within the rules as er set out by the Guinness Book of Records.
I Are you the first person to have tried to do this?
T.B. Absolutely yeah. Yes, I was um . . . the first person to achieve it.
I What made you want to do it?
T.B. Um . . . it was just it seemed like a er . . . such a challenge that once I'd got the idea in my head um . . . I couldn't let it go, and windsurfing's a funny sport because when you start it seems the most unlikely method of transport you could imagine. Um . . . when you, when you find that you can actually move quite consistently in one direction you're so surprised that you . . . you know, it's sort of revelatory and I thought um . . . when I, when I started to get reasonably good at it, I thought wouldn't it be interesting to try and go a really long distance on this –how about going around Britain and er . . . 18 months later I set off.
I Did you need sponsorship? or . . .
T.B. Oh yes. It, er . . . the whole trip cost about 35,000 and I raised that money from a champagne company in the end, a French champagne company.
I Looking back, how do you view the experience?
T.B. Um . . . I think it's the best thing that I have ever done um . . . the thing I'll probably be most proud of and um . . . you know until my dying day.
I Was it worth it then for you?
T.B. Oh, god yes, I would do it again any time. In fact um . . .I do keep on doing it again er . . . it is one of the regular dreams I've had over the two years since I did it is that I am um . . . doing it again and I um . . . and each time . . . each dream is the same. I'm always going um . . . anticlockwise, this time, I went clockwise and I'm always doing it again and I can't understand why I'm doing it. Why am I doing this again, I say to myself in my dreams.
I So have you any plans for any um . . . other events like this?
T.B. I've flirted with the idea of er . . . windsurfing around the world um . . . when I got back, but decided that um . . . 30,000 miles would probably be a little bit harder than the 2,000 that I've just done and er . . . thought that there were probably safer ways of seeing the world.

UNIT 6

We've been looking at types of behaviour in different societies, and today we're going to take a look at the Subanun people of the Philippines.

To start with, a few words about Subanun society. We might consider it rather odd that there are no positions or offices which automatically give the holder authority over others, that is to say, no equivalent of posts such as judge. Decisions are made by those who can demonstrate their ability to do so in social encounters, for example a drinking encounter, which we'll be hearing about in a minute. This ability depends on the amount of deference one receives from other participants in the encounter. No external status attributes, like age, sex or wealth are sufficient to guarantee deference.

So let's see how this works in the drinking encounter. How can society be organized without people like judges and police officers to tell you what you can and can't do? We might divide the encounter into three stages, namely the initial tasting stage, followed by competitive drinking and finally the game-drinking stage.

In the opening stage, talk consists largely of inviting someone to drink and asking permission to drink. The provider of the beer invites another to drink and in this way defers to that person. That person in turn can create other role-relations by inviting others to drink. The order in which he invites people and the terms of address he uses to each can then define the various role-relations.

As competitive drinking begins, talk shifts to the beer itself, its taste, strength and so on, and the performance of the various drinkers is evaluated. Here it is not what is said that is important, that is relatively predictable, but the response of others to what you say. Little reaction or encouragement from the other participants means that particular person will drop out at this stage. And in fact the encounter is normally reduced to about half a dozen.

As the role-structure, that is who defers to whom, becomes defined, talk moves on to relatively trivial gossip and then proceeds to discussion of more important subjects of current interest. And in many cases it is at this stage that decisions may be made of the sort a judge would normally make. The decision will be finally made, and even a fine imposed, by the individual who achieved a commanding role in the encounter through talk.

If drinking continues long enough, the focus shifts from topics to the message forms themselves. In other words, a game is made of the use of language. Songs and verses are composed on the spot, and decision-making may continue but this time on the basis of this verbal artistry. This also helps to ensure that the festivity will end with good feelings among all participants.

UNIT 7

Defence (*rising*) You are Mabel Laurentina Groomkirby?

Mabel Yes, sir.

Defence You are the mother of the accused, Mrs Groomkirby, are you not?

Mabel Oh, well, yes. I suppose if it's Kirby on trial, I must be. I hadn't realized.

Defence It would be true to say, wouldn't it, Mrs Groomkirby, that your son likes wearing black?

Mabel He's worn it all his life.

Defence He likes wearing black but he doesn't feel justified in wearing it except at the funeral of someone he knows?

Mabel Well, it's only in the last few years he's come to think like that, really. He always used to just wear it.

Defence His attitude has changed?

Mabel It's been very noticeable over the last year or two.

Defence Can you account for this change in any way, Mrs Groomkirby?

Mabel Not really – unless his studies have had anything to do with it. He's always been of a very logical turn of mind ever since he was born, but what with all this studying lately he seems to have got a different attitude altogether these last few years.

Defence Your son is a rather ingenious young man, is he not, Mrs Groomkirby?

Mabel A lot of people say he is, yes, sir.

Defence He has a cash register, I believe.

Mabel That's right.

Defence What exactly is the function of this cash register, Mrs Groomkirby? What does your son use it for?

Mabel It was an egg-timer to begin with, and then he gradually came to rely on it more and more for other things.

Defence When it was an egg-timer – can you tell his Lordship how it worked.

Mabel Well, sir, it was rigged up in the kitchen with the telephone on one side of it and the gas stove on the other. He likes to have his eggs done the exact time –just the four minutes ten seconds – or he won't eat them. He just goes right inside himself. So he rigged up the cash register.

Defence How did it work, Mrs Groomkirby?

Mabel He'd got a stop-watch but he wouldn't trust that. He'd trust it for the minutes but he wouldn't trust it for the seconds.

Defence And so he used the cash register instead?

Mabel That and the telephone. He had them side by side.

Defence What was the actual procedure he adopted, Mrs Groomkirby?

Mabel Well, he'd put his egg on to boil, then he'd stand there with his stop-watch.

Defence Go on, Mrs Groomkirby.

Mabel Well, then the moment it said four minutes exactly on his stop-watch, he'd simply dial TIM, wait for the pips, ring up No Sale on the cash register and take out his egg.

Defence And this was, in fact, the only sequence of actions that took precisely the ten seconds.

Mabel That's right, sir. He wouldn't eat them otherwise.

Defence And he worked this out for himself without any assistance whatever from anyone else.

Mabel Oh, yes. It was entirely his own.

Defence You say your son, Mrs Groomkirby, has always liked wearing black. Will you tell his Lordship in your own words about this attachment to black clothes?

Mabel Well, sir, all his baby things were black. We got it all planned before he was born that if we had a white baby we were going to dress him in black – or her in black if it had been a girl – and if either of them were black we'd have everything white, so as to make a contrast. But when he came he was white so we had the black.

Judge (*intervening*) Is your husband a coloured man, Mrs Groomkirby?

Mabel He's an insurance agent, sir.

Judge Yes, but is he coloured?

Mabel Well, no, sir. Not so far as I know.

Judge What I'm trying to get from you, Mrs Groomkirby, is the simple fact of your husband's racial characteristics. Does he, for instance, have any negro blood?

Mabel Well – he *has* got one or two bottles up in his room, but he doesn't tell me what's in them.

Defence There's one more thing I should like to ask you, Mrs Groomkirby. Each of your son's forty-three victims was struck with an iron bar after having been told a joke. Would it be true to say that your son, Mrs Groomkirby, went to considerable trouble over these jokes?

Mabel He went to very great trouble indeed, sir. He sat up to all hours thinking out jokes for them.

Defence Can you tell his Lordship why your son went to all this trouble with every one of his forty-three victims, when there were a number of far simpler methods he could have used?

Mabel I think for one thing he rather took to the humorous side of it. And for another thing he always wanted to do everything he could for these people. He felt very sorry for them.

Defence He wanted to make things as pleasant as possible for them even at some considerable trouble and inconvenience to himself?

Mabel He didn't mind how much trouble he went to, as long as they ended on a gay note.

Defence Thank you, Mrs Groomkirby.

UNIT 8

Good evening. Here is the news:

Secret talks are taking place at official levels to make reality of a dream which has captured the imagination on both sides of the Atlantic since 1776; the wounds that have divided the two nations will at last be healed. It will be the most remarkable diplomatic and political achievement since the Declaration of Independence. The plan has been denied by Downing Street, but reliable diplomatic sources have confirmed the reunion. US Senators favour the scheme which will give them, they hope, real aristocratic titles such as those granted to members of the House of Lords, while British public opinion, it is feared, will oppose the project. 'What,' ask Britons, 'is in it for us?'

A leading American scientist warned in an interview on American television last night that a nuclear holocaust could be sparked off by accident. This was denied by a government spokesman who claimed all measures had been taken to avoid such an eventuality.

The American multi-millionaire oil tycoon J. R. Schwarzenburger the Third Junior has made a spectacular bid to purchase Greece's most famous classical monument, the Parthenon. The Greek government, Mr Schwarzenburger is quoted as saying, will find his offer hard to turn down: the Parthenon, he added, will look 'just swell' in Beverley Hills.

The world's leading transplant surgeon, Dr Christopher Bernard, has carried out one of the most difficult brain tissue transplants yet attempted. The South African surgeon has succeeded in transplanting tissues into the human brain in what is thought to be the first operation of its kind. The surgery was performed a week ago on a patient suffering from Parkinson's disease. A portion of the patient's adrenal gland was implanted into a part of the patient's brain, an operation which has previously been performed only on rats and monkeys.

And now a look at the weather . . .

UNIT 9

1

A Good evening, I'm calling on behalf of the World Wildlife Fund, and I'd like to tell you a bit about our work – it'll only take a moment.

B Oh all right.

A Our task is to help preserve life in the natural world.

B Oh.

A Take birds, for example. A rare species of goose, the Néné, had been reduced to fewer than 50.

B I see.

A But with the help of the Wildfowl Trust in England, 700 were raised from a few captive pairs.

B Really.

A And thanks to the World Wildlife Fund, 200 of these were flown back to Hawaii, which is their natural habitat. And they're thriving once more.

B Very interesting.

A Perhaps, therefore, you would like to aid our efforts by making a contribution.

2

A Hallo, I'm calling on behalf of the World Wildlife Fund.

B The what?

A The World Wildlife Fund. If you've got a few minutes I'd like to tell you what that means.

B Oh, all right.

A We work to conserve natural areas that contain endangered wildlife. The seas, for example, have become polluted by the industrialized world; whales are being hunted to extinction; turtles are rolled off their eggs when they come ashore to breed or are slaughtered for their meat and oil . . .

B Oh.

A Crocodiles are killed to make handbags and shoes; Walruses are hunted for their ivory.

B I see.

A Seals are bludgeoned to death to provide fur coats and the threat of extinction hangs over several species of whale, dolphin and porpoise.

B Really.

A We are now campaigning to provide sea sanctuaries for some of these endangered species.

B Very interesting.

A Aided by our campaign, protected nesting sites for turtles have already been set up. As you can see, this is very valuable work and I wonder therefore if you'd like to make a donation?

3

A Hallo, I'm calling on behalf of the World Wildlife Fund. I'd like to tell you just a little bit about our work.

B Oh all right.

A We work to conserve nature. For instance 50 years ago there were 100,000 tigers in the world but today there are not more than 5,000 left.

B Oh.

A To save the tiger we launched Operation Tiger and as a result there are now reserves in India and Nepal and conservation projects in several other countries.

B I see.

A Thanks to our campaign many women now feel embarrassed to appear in furs and fashion magazines agreed not to advertise the furs of endangered animals.

B Really.

A Through our efforts several countries have imposed export bans on the furs of endangered species, and Britain, the United States and Canada have put controls on importation.

B Mm, very interesting.

A I wonder if you would like to support this valuable work by making a contribution?

UNIT 10

The men gave a shout of triumph. They saw, as they imagined, their enemies in flight, and they rushed after them in disorder. This was just what Snowball had intended. As soon as they were well inside the yard, the three horses, the three cows, and the rest of the pigs, who had been lying in ambush in the cowshed, suddenly emerged in their rear, cutting them off. Snowball now gave the signal for the charge. He himself dashed straight for Jones. Jones saw him coming, raised his gun, and fired. The pellets scored bloody streaks along Snowball's back, and a sheep dropped dead. Without halting for an instant Snowball flung his fifteen stone against Jones's legs. Jones was hurled into a pile of dung and his gun flew out of his hands. But the most terrifying spectacle of all was Boxer, rearing up on his hind legs and striking out with his great iron-shod hoofs like a stallion. His very first blow took a stable-lad from Foxwood on the skull and stretched him lifeless in the mud. At the sight, several men dropped their sticks and tried to run. Panic overtook them, and the next moment all the animals together were chasing them round and round the yard. They were gored, kicked, bitten, trampled on. There was not an animal on the farm that did not take vengeance on them after his own fashion. Even the cat suddenly leapt off a roof on to a cowman's shoulders and sank her claws in his neck, at which he yelled horribly. At a moment when the opening was clear, the men were glad enough to rush out of the yard and make a bolt for the main road. And so within five minutes of their invasion they were in ignominious retreat by the same way as they had come, with a flock of geese hissing after them and pecking at their calves all the way.

UNIT 11

See page 55 for the poem *Me and the Animals*.

UNIT 12

Presenter Judging from our mailbag, our programme on animal welfare last week seems to have hit a sensitive spot. Mr G. Randall writes:

Voice 1 With regard to the welfare of animals I must say I am confused on the issue. On the one hand we are asked to contribute to societies who work to preserve rare species from extinction, and on the other hand we are expected to agree with the mass slaughter of animals in laboratories for obscure scientific purposes. I would hate to think that those species saved at such cost from extinction are later to be fed to the laboratories. We are expected to believe and it may well be true that science does not inflict pain unnecessarily but surely the issue is not pain but life itself. If we work so hard to conserve life in some areas of the animal kingdom, does this give us the right to take life elsewhere?

Presenter And Ms E. Sharp had this to say:

Voice 2 I am amazed at all this fuss about animals. To discuss the use of animals in experiments is all very well, but at what point do you draw the line? No doubt many listeners keep pets and think nothing of taking their children to the circus. Are they not therefore contributing to the exploitation of animals? Would they refuse to allow their daughters to go horse-riding? Blood sports are also often cited as examples of our cruelty to animals, but the hunting of one species by another originates in the animal kingdom itself, where it helps to preserve the balance of nature. If I had to choose between the life of a young rabbit and the life of a young child, I would not find my decision difficult.

UNIT 13

Picture 1

For me, it's . . . it's the grace with which the animal moves. Such delicate-looking legs and . . . and yet they can carry all that weight over those huge fences. I think it's a beautiful sight. Can't think of any other sport like it, really. And it doesn't harm anyone, does it?

Picture 2

I think there's no finer sight than a person in full flight. It's great to see human beings performing at the peak of their mental and physical fitness. I get a real thrill when I see them sprinting for all they're worth round that last bend in the track. Just because I'm a bit of a wreck myself doesn't stop me appreciating what others can do.

Picture 3

I go for a good old yell, I do. I'm stuck at home all week so it's great to be able to get out and have a good shout —releases the frustration, doesn't it? Sometimes I'd like to get in the ring with them and have a good kick and scratch and pull their hair out. Well, it serves them right, doesn't it, two grown men carrying on like that.

Picture 4

I don't care what's happening on the pitch, it's the terraces I'm interested in. You've got to use a lot of skill to work yourself into a position where you can attack the other fans. Well, they're the enemy, aren't they? They're in our territory and we've got to defend it. It's pretty boring working in a bank, you know.

UNIT 14

Exercise 3a

1 Cricket began in the 17th century, didn't it?
2 Cricket didn't begin in the 17th century, did it?
3 Cricket began in the 17th century, didn't it?
4 Cricket didn't begin the 17th century, did it?

Exercise 3b

1 Cricket isn't male-dominated, is it?
2 Cricket's male-dominated, isn't it?
3 Cricket isn't male-dominated, is it?
4 Cricket's male-dominated, isn't it?

Exercise 3c

1 We can't learn anything about a society from its sports, can we?
2 The origins of cricket are rather controversial, aren't they?
3 It was the aristocrats who started it all, wasn't it?
4 They never used to gamble on games though, did they?
5 And that was why they created the professional player, wasn't it?
6 But these professionals weren't professional in the way we mean nowadays, were they?
7 I mean, they had another job, apart from playing cricket, didn't they?
8 Things didn't really change much during industrialization, did they?
9 But popular recreation wasn't really transformed to suit the dictates of industry, was it?
10 Anyway the professional player is much better off these days, isn't he?

Exercise 4

Janice Well, we've heard about the part that patronage played in the development of cricket. Let's hear now from some of those intimately involved in the popular game of tennis. Bob, you've coached some of our best young players, have you noticed any changes in the game?

Bob I think it's fair to say sport is now big business, and this has meant changes.

Janice Right. Mac, as a top player now for several years, what changes have you noticed?

Mac Well, the odd regulation or two, Janice, but . . .

Bob No, more than that, Mac. The desire to win, often at all costs, is more and more evident nowadays.

Janice Yes, surely we're living in a world where success is at a premium.

Bob And this has meant, as the pressure and the prize money increases, that standards of behaviour have declined.

Janice Jane, you lecture on physical education, what do you think?

Jane Well . . . erm, I agree with Bob.

Bob There's a growing tendency to challenge the umpire's decisions.

Jane Exactly. I feel this influence of money on sport needs to be checked and broken. It's an unhealthy trend.*

Mac But you'd take away enjoyment for so many. What about the kids who dream of becoming big sport stars?

Bob But how many make it, Mac? Oh, it's all very well for you or I to talk but what of the thousands who don't make the grade?

Jane Yes, they're thrown back into the routine of factory or office life, disenchanted and disillusioned.

Mac But these kids couldn't live without their idols. And at least there's an outside chance of fame and fortune.

Jane Do we need professional sportspeople at all?

Mac Pardon?

Jane There we are, pouring millions into commercial sponsorship, while facilities offered in schools are falling all the time. We badly need a new sense of sporting and recreational priorities.

Mac What do you mean, we don't need professional sportspeople?

Janice Well . . . Should there be this divorce between the professional and the community?

Jane If the working week were reduced, then leisure time would become more significant. And access to recreational facilities would be more widely available.

Bob Sport for all!

Janice And on that note, I'm afraid, we'll have to finish.

Mac But, I haven't said what I . . .

Janice Sorry, Mac. It's time for a short commercial break.

Mac I don't believe this . . .

UNIT 15

This European Cup Final has been quite a match – Wigan United have fought like lions to hang on to the championship. Now with just one minute to go it looks like they're going to make it. And a lot of the credit must go to winger Johnny Bull who fired the winning shot in the 30th minute. Up front, Harry Wharton and Bob Cherry have been launching attack after attack, while Frank Nugent and Vernon Smith have been as solid as rocks in defence. But the whole team have played like heroes. Billy Bunter in goal has had an absolutely fantastic game beating away a free kick touched by Piccoli to Riviera. And now the referee's looking at his watch as the entire Italian team crowds into the Wigan penalty area, but really the battle is over and with only seconds to go Piccoli shoots . . . yes . . . no . . . it's all over . . . !!

UNIT 16

Oh, yes she can outrun every competitor in her class. She can also withstand the greatest tests of endurance and stamina, she just runs and runs hour after hour. Yes, I reckon she's got the endurance to win.

UNIT 17

Extract 1

F So you are unmarried, as well as famous.

M Famous because I'm unmarried.

F And courteous because of which?

M Either one you like.

F Well, frankly, I prefer courtesy.

M Mm. Do you often get it?

F Always . . . eventually. Don't you believe in marriage?

M Yes, as long as there are no women in it. You don't like me, do you?

F Oh, I like anyone who believes there may be something he doesn't know.

M What do you mean by that?

Extract 2 (a few minutes later)

F Isn't it funny, we both thought of moving at the same time. You take mine and I'll take yours.

M You bitch.

F What made you say that?

M You know why I said that.

F It's funny how few men know that women like to be talked to that way.

M I am not like other men.

F Why doesn't George come for me! Isn't it boring, waiting for someone?

M Yes. Who is George, may I ask?

F Certainly you may ask.
M Well, who is he? I had gathered you were pining for the late lamented.
F The late lamented?
M That fox-faced Henry or Oswald or something.
F Oh, Donald. Do you mean Donald?
M Surely. Let him be Donald then.
F Do you know, you are impossible.

Extract 3

M All right. So I am, but then I wasn't engaged to Donald. And George is not calling for me.
F What makes you so angry? Because I won't let you put your hands on me?
M My dear woman, if I had wanted to put my hands on you I would have done it.
F Yes?
M Certainly. Don't you believe it?
F I don't know . . . but what good would it do to you?
M No good at all. That's the reason I don't want to.
F Why do you tell yourself lies?
M Same reason you do.
F I?
M Surely. You intend to kiss me and yet you are going to all this damn trouble about it.
F Do you know, I believe I hate you.
M I don't doubt it. I know damn well I hate you.

UNIT 18

I=Interviewer, M=Minister.

I Do you really think your bill will manage to do away with inequality between the sexes?
M We have managed with the new bill to achieve legal equality; therefore it is more correct to speak of equality of rights. The two sexes are equal before the law. Real equality is something that has to do with social realities and that cannot be achieved from one moment to the next by laws. The law helps of course, but it cannot solve the problem.
I In the previous law, if the wife owned property as part of her dowry, she retained the right of ownership, but the husband had the right to administer the property – has this been done away with?
M Yes. Now the wife both owns and administers her property.
I What happens in the case of divorce – does the husband still have to pay alimony to his ex-wife?
M It depends. The ex-wife may have to pay alimony to the ex-husband. If the husband isn't in a position to support himself, if he cannot earn enough money to take care of himself, the ex-wife may be obliged to support him. It now works both ways.
I So alimony and child support will continue to exist, but will have to be paid by the one who has the greatest economic means?
M Precisely.

I Also in the previous law – and this was of special concern to foreign wives – there was a provision that said if the wife wanted to travel abroad with the children this required the written permission of the husband – does this still hold?
M This is really a matter for the Foreign Ministry, but as far as we are concerned it no longer applies. No. It has been replaced by common consent. It may still require the signature of the partner who remains behind, whether this is the husband or the wife.
I I see. And to go back to the dowry – is this still obligatory in cases where the parents have property?
M No. It is purely voluntary . . . in practice of course this may present problems . . .

UNIT 19

1

Nurse She was lucky really – it's just a broken leg. She wants to see you. Would you like to follow me?

2

Diana Chuck, how sweet of you to wait!
Chuck You knew I'd wait. How are you feeling?

3

Chuck There's quite a crowd in there – I guess I'll come back another day.

4

Chuck You're all on your own! I can hardly believe my luck.
Diana You're the only visitor I've had all day.

5

Chuck They must be crazy to stay away from you, Diana. I'd spend every day here if I could.
Diana Everybody else seems to have better ways of passing their time – they've just lost interest in me.

6

Chuck Hi, Di, how are you feeling today? In the mood for a little music?
Diana Oh Chuck that's really cute of you. I'd just love to hear some music.

7

Diana You've been so good to me, Chuck. You're so . . . reliable. I don't know how to thank you . . .

UNIT 20

I Hallo again. In today's 'Women's Half-Hour' we take a look at the disquieting increase in the incidence of attacks against women and we ask: is there anything women themselves can do about it? Here to discuss the question with me are Anna Rowbotham, a housewife and Mary Mitchell who is a member of the 'Four Seasons' folk group. Anna and Mary are both students of what most people would regard as an exclusively male sport: karate. Anna, what was it that made you take up karate?

A Well, it was just that I felt I'd gone to pieces physically after having two children. There were so many jobs I just wasn't considered suitable for, because I was a woman and therefore supposed to be weak. So I thought of strength, not really in terms of being able to fight but in order to work, to lift heavy boxes, pick up heavy objects. I had always been seen as someone frail. It was so frustrating . . .

I So your aim was purely practical . . .

A Yes, I decided to do something about it.

I Mary Mitchell, why did you learn self-defence . . . why karate?

M I live alone in a flat. I used to be petrified to undress and go to bed at night. As for having a bath – that was unthinkable. I was terrified of someone breaking into the flat. I was never afraid in the street, only when I came home; so it was for self-protection that I took up karate . . .

I You felt vulnerable . . .

M At home yes.

I Anna, did you feel insecure?

A Well, not at home as much as in the street. I always felt nervous coming home late or just out shopping. I'd had enough of being hassled by strangers, and worrying about being beaten up, you know, wondering whether someone was going to leap out at me from some dark corner . . .

I And has karate changed the way you feel as women?

A Oh, yes, absolutely.

I Mary?

M Yes. Tremendously. Karate has affected my attitude towards my body. I always felt pressured into hiding . . . well, my size. You know, stooping and scrupulously avoiding skirts. The extraordinary thing is I now accept and use my height. I no longer feel tall and awkward.

I Anna, in what way has karate changed your . . . experience . . .

A Well, for one thing it's stopped me panicking. I would go all numb. I think I can now face confrontation without freezing like a scared rabbit. I'm not afraid of being bothered in the street anymore. When I went to Paris with my sister a couple of weeks ago we were constantly being hassled. I said to one of the men: 'I'll hit you,' and he said he'd love it. I slapped him and he thrust himself at me and then it became a complete brawl. I fought badly, but eventually he ran away, petrified. He dropped his packet of Gauloises. We had a moral victory anyway.

I So what advice would you give to women who feel vulnerable? What should they do if attacked?

A Well, I don't think violence should be used indiscriminately, and anyway karate takes time. You've got to learn the techniques. So I'd say if you think you're going to be attacked, start running and don't scream. Shout. If you can, carry a whistle and blow hard. Make as much noise as you can.

I What if you can't get away – if say he grabs you from behind . . .

M I'd concentrate on kicking him: kick low and hard. Aim at his shins and kneecaps – that's where it hurts. Better still, bend your knees, lower yourself right down, then bend right forward and jerk your hips to one side. That should fling him off. It's difficult, but effective.

I Well, on that energetic note, we must stop. Thank you both for coming. It's been very informative. Now it's time for this week's serial . . .

UNIT 22

Studies of the human brain have revealed some indications of how this important organ might have evolved over millions of years. The ancient Greeks were aware that the human brain was divided into several separate structures, or brains, each of which apparently had specific functions. In the area where the spinal cord enters the brain, for example, the cord widens into a structure sometimes identified by the medical term of *medulla oblongata*, and sometimes called simply the hindbrain. This is the sort of brain found in some very primitive animals that possess a spinal cord of any sort. Located next to the hindbrain in humans and more advanced types of animals with a spinal cord is a bulge of brain tissue known as the *cerebellum*, or little brain.

UNIT 24

See page 126 for the poem *The Unknown Citizen*.

UNIT 25

See page 133.

UNIT 26

1st witch When shall we three meet again
In thunder, lightning or in rain?
2nd witch When the hurlyburly's done
When the battle's lost and won.
3rd witch That will be ere the set of sun.
1st witch Where the place?
2nd witch Upon the heath.
3rd witch There to meet with Macbeth.
1st witch I come, Greymalkin!
2nd witch Paddock calls.
3rd witch Anon.
All Fair is foul, and foul is fair
Hover through the fog and filthy air.
(later)
3rd witch A drum! a drum!
Macbeth doth come.
All The weird sisters, hand in hand,
Posters of the sea and land
Thus do go about, about:
Thrice to thine, and thrice to mine,
And thrice again, to make up nine.
Peace! The charm's wound up.
Macbeth So foul and fair a day I have not seen.
Banquo How far is't called to Forres? What are these,
So withered and so wild in their attire,
That look not like th' inhabitants o'the earth
And yet are on't? Live you? Or are you aught
That man may question? You seem to understand me,
By each at once her choppy finger laying
Upon her skinny lips: you should be women,
And yet your beards forbid me to interpret
That you are so.

UNIT 27

Exercise 2a
V=Vistor, H=Human

V . . . and that's my job. Fun, isn't it?
H It's amazing.
V Unfortunately I got stuck on earth for rather longer than I intended.
H Intended?
V Yes, I only planned to stay for a week but I got stuck for fifteen years.
H But how did you get here in the first place?
V Easy, I got a lift from a teaser.
H A teaser?
V Yeah.
H Er, what's a . . .
V Teasers are usually rich kids with nothing to do. Anyway, they cruise around in their modulars . . .
H Modulars?
V Er, what do you call them – spaceships. As I was saying, they cruise around looking for planets which haven't made interstellar contact yet and buzz them.
H Buzz them?
V Yeah, they buzz them. They find some isolated spot with very few people around, then land right by some poor unsuspecting soul whom no one's ever going to believe and then strut up and down in front of him wearing silly antennae on their head and making beep beep noises . . .
H Oh, so all those reports about UFOs . . .
V Rather childish really.

Exercise 2c
H So you got here by hitch-hiking.
H Yes, you got a lift from a rich brat.
H One of those spoilt kids, you said, who cruise around in their spaceships.
H Modulars I think you called them. And these kids are always doing silly pranks.
H Like buzzing we poor humans.
H What would you call us – earth beings? Anyway you've certainly got an odd occupation.
H I think it'd be a good idea if you took some more English lessons. Have you got the First Certificate?
H Oh never mind!

UNIT 28

I=Interviewer, F=Frankenstein

I Well, Mr Frankenstein – er . . . would it be all right if I called you Frank?

F Call me what you like – most people do.

I Well, Frank, it has been said, and I . . . I don't want to give offence but one does often hear the comment that you're a bit of a, well, how shall I put it, a bit of a monster.

F That's a lot of nonsense, that is.

I I wonder if you could, well, elaborate a little?

F I'm no more of a monster than you are.

I Well I can be rather beastly at times.

F Yeah, so your assistant was telling me. Anyway, the point is, remarks like that make me really wild. You people are all the same, you are. You're intolerant of anybody who's a bit different. I mean, a little strange I may be, but a monster I am not.

I Well I wonder if you'd mind telling me about your neighbours, I mean how do you get on with them?

F Not very well, to tell the truth. They're a weird lot, they are. Take the house next door. Now I never actually see anyone going in or out, I just hear them.

I That's rather odd isn't it?

F It's always at night. Last night I heard a car arriving, you know, tyres crunching on the gravel, then a door slamming, then I heard lots of creaking floorboards, muttering and cursing and what sounded like furniture being moved. Then there was lots of wailing.

I Well I must admit, that does sound rather odd.

F And then opposite you've got three old girls. Now they've got some funny habits, they have.

I Oh, like what?

F Well for a start, they've got hundreds of cats. Black they are, every one of them. And about once a year they have a sort of party. Sabbath, they call it, but I know what I call it.

I What?

F Orgies, that's what they are.

I But surely three harmless little old ladies fond of cats wouldn't . . .

F Don't you believe it. There's something sinister about them. And I really can't understand a word they say either. Always talking in sort of rhymes they are.

I Well er have you got any other interesting neighbours?

F Well there's the bloke on the other side.

I I wonder if you could tell us a little about him.

F Not much to tell really. Doesn't seem to do a lot –out of work he says he is. Drinks a bit now and then –had a spot of trouble with the police once or twice. Bit of a dreamer, if you ask me, always staring into space he is, but apart from that really he's all right. Only normal one on the street, frankly.

I Well it's been extremely interesting to have the opportunity to talk to you. Thank you for coming along.

F Oh, is that it then?

UNIT 29

1 I'm sorry; I didn't see the sign. I just wanted to pop into the chemist's for some aspirins – I'll be more careful in future.

2 He will forgive you. He forgives all our trespasses. It's not too late to change; trust Him, believe in Him. Ask for forgiveness.

3 We will create jobs, build houses and schools, we shall put the economy back on its feet and make this country great again.

4 Darling, I don't know how to put this. Do you think we could . . . I mean . . . you know how fond I am of you . . . would you . . . will you darling . . . shall we . . .?

UNIT 30

1

A Hallo, back again?

B Yes, just popped in to pick up those books.

A I wonder if you'd mind closing the door.

B Oh yes – I'm terribly sorry. I'm always doing that, aren't I?

2

A Oh, hallo, James – you wanted to see me?

B Yes, that's right, come on in.

A What, what's it all about?

B It's rather confidential, actually.

A Oh, I'll er, close the door then, shall I?

B Good. Now it's about that new secretary of yours, you know, the one who . . .

3

A Excuse me sir.

B Yes, what is it?

A Er, can I talk to you for a moment?

B Yes, I suppose so. Come in.

A Thank you sir. Well it's about the exam . . .

B Were you born in a barn?

A Oh, sorry sir. Well, as you know, the boy sitting next to me . . .

4

A The tulips will bloom in June.
Z Enter.
B Erm . . . the tulips will bloom in June.
Z Enter.
C The tulips will bloom in June.
Z Enter.
D The tulips will bloom in June.
Z Enter. Well . . . I think everybody is here.

5

A Right here we are then. Out you get.
B It seems to be stuck.
A Oh, let me have a go. There we are.
B Oh, yes. Well, 'bye then, and thanks.
A Don't mention it. Enjoy your holiday. 'Bye.

UNIT 31

TENDEREX. So soft and tender, because it's the only toilet tissue that gives you that very special soothing softness, that TENDEREX super softness. And only TENDEREX gives you and your whole family that fresh, relaxing feeling. They'll welcome the gentleness of the softest, tenderest toilet tissue. Next time you shop, ask for TENDEREX in any of five fresh colours.

UNIT 32

Instructor All right, I think we're ready for the real thing now. But before we get out there, let's just get one or two things clear – rules of the road, sort of thing. If you happen to fall over, don't lie there all day. The idea is to keep the piste clear, so get up and out of the way. Whatever you do, don't try getting up with your skis pointing downhill.
Pupil 1 Is it more difficult like that?
Instructor Don't you remember. Somebody, tell him.
Pupil 2 You'll start moving downhill before you're ready.*
Instructor That's it. Now if you're going to change direction or stop, mind you don't cross someone else's path. In other words . . .
Pupil 2 Look behind you.
Instructor Right.
Pupil 1 Erm . . . what if you're skiing too fast – you know, out of control?
Pupil 3 Ski into deeper snow to slow down.
Instructor Just a minute. That's exactly what you don't do. That's a good way to break a leg. Mind you stay on the piste at all times. If you're out of control, fall over, in the way you were shown. Now if you hear the cry 'Piste' in some foreign accent, that'll be some speed merchant trying to get past. It's no good panicking – keep calm, slow down and let him pass.

Pupil 1 Erm . . . don't you shout 'ski'?
Instructor And what do you shout if your ski comes off and goes hurtling down the slope: 'piste'!?
Pupil 1 Oh, yeah, sorry.
Instructor We'll stick to the drag lift today. Now if you manage to fall going up that, let go. It's pointless hanging on because you'll never get to your feet again. So let go and scramble out of the way as best you can. And remember of course to check your bindings are OK before skiing off.
Pupil 1 Bindings?
Instructor Oh dear! Yes, the things that hold your boots to your skis!
Pupil 1 Oh yeah, bindings.
Instructor Right, that's enough chat – let's get on with it. Watch out for this ice outside the door here. Oh! (crash) Oh no, my leg!

UNIT 33

It is perhaps easy enough to identify good ecological reasons why animals should migrate, and even to appreciate that the timing of migrations might be determined by environmental cues such as changing day-length or temperature. The real mystery that has baffled scientist and non-scientist alike over the centuries has been how the migrants know which way to go. To arrive at a pinpoint in the middle of an uncharted ocean is no mean feat for human navigators, even with modern satellite navigation systems to hand. That 'mere' animals can achieve the same without the advantage of even the crudest sextant or compass seems little short of miraculous.

UNIT 34

T.A.=Travel Agent, M=Man, W=Woman

T.A. Good morning, can I help you?
M Yes, we'd like a holiday.
T.A. Good, that's what we're here for. Anywhere in particular?
M Somewhere with no irregular verbs.*
T.A. Mm, that *might* be just a little difficult. Of course, there is always Albania.
W Albania?
T.A. Yes, they don't allow anything irregular there. Not that there's a great deal to do there, I'm afraid.
W Oh that *does* sound exciting.
T.A. Um . . . it's not really noted for its excitement.
M Well can you suggest anywhere else. We've been to most places, you see.
W I suppose you *have* got some exciting holidays.
T.A. How about camel-trekking in Oman?
M Well, I don't think I fancy that – we went on a camel in Cairo. Bad-tempered thing, it was – it spat at me.
T.A. How strange.
M So I spat right back at it.
W And I hit it with my handbag.
T.A. Well, in that case perhaps Oman is not for you. Um . . . I know I've got just the place – Spain!
W Spain! That would be nice!
M We've been there.
W Six times.
T.A. But there are a thousand Spains to visit!
M It didn't mention that in the brochure.
W I thought there was only one – down at the bottom of France.
T.A. One country, but any number of holidays! For example, you can laze all day on a secluded beach.
M Well, I *do* like beaches. All those bikinis!
W I don't really care for them.
T.A. And the beaches of Spain are renowned for their . . . er . . . endless variety. Or travel inland and journey through history. Countless castles dot the landscape and you can even stay in them – some are now hotels.
W Well that *could* be a bit different, I suppose.
T.A. Or you might care to do a little shopping. Spanish leather for example is of the very best quality and very reasonably priced.
M Oh I *am* fond of a spot of bargain-hunting.
W It *does* sound a bit more varied than the average holiday.
T.A. And after a morning's shopping, a refreshing glass of wine – there are many different wines to sample.
M Any music?
T.A. Ah, the music of Spain will have you stamping your feet to its pulsating rhythm. And everywhere you go you will be met by the traditional hospitality and courtesy of Spain.
W Er . . . where do *you* normally go for your holidays?
T.A. Well, camel-trekking in Oman, actually – there are just too many British tourists everywhere else.

UNIT 35

I=Interviewer, S=Severin

Part 1

I Why have you chosen to recreate this particular voyage?
S Well, as you know my main concern is to investigate the er . . . investigation of legends and myths about voyages and to try and distinguish between the two: what is purely completely invented – myth, and what is based on fact . . .
I For this voyage you've actually reconstructed the Argo, the boat in which Jason and the Argonauts actually sailed – I mean, does it work?
S Oh yes, it works as well as any modern racing yacht and it's real – it's actually a replica of a Greek galley, a Bronze Age galley.
I It must've taken some time to build.
S Not really. Some people said it would take up to at least three years but we finished it in just six months in fact.

Part 2

I Tim, you have in fact reconstructed other er . . . legendary voyages. This isn't your first.
S Yes we did the Sindbad voyage a few years ago.
I Sindbad the Sailor – the Arabian Nights?
S That's right, for that one we set off from Muscat, navigated the Indian Ocean and the South China Sea. What we were doing was erm trying to recreate the voyages of Sindbad to check their authenticity. It was the same on the Brendan voyage, he was an Irish monk who lived in the 6th Century – I reconstructed the boat from medieval documents er tried to reproduce medieval materials and technology.
I And what were you trying to prove . . .
S That St Brendan could've crossed from the Kerry Coast to the New World in a boat made locally . . .
I . . . a thousand years before Columbus?
S Exactly.
I This time you're going to try and retrace the route taken by Jason and the Argonauts . . .
S Yes we're heading for Georgia in the Soviet Union – from Spetses we go to Volos and then we'll head for the Dardanelles into the sea of Marmara and then across the Black Sea Coast of Northern Turkey.
I How long will the voyage last?
S About three and a half months.

UNIT 36

Crowd Where are they? I can see them. Yes, that's them. Here they come. Now, we agreed I'd ask first, OK?

Crowd Mr Robertson . . . Can you tell us . . . A word . . .

Dougal Hey, hey, hang on a moment. We're not used to all this. We'll answer your questions of course, just . .

Journalist 1 How did you manage in such a small boat?

Dougal Oh, well, er . . . storms were a problem of course. I was afraid we'd flood or overturn.

Neil We had one really bad storm didn't we, Dad?

Dougal Yeah, we were exhausted by the end of it.

Lyn But storms also meant water, which we were desperate for.

Dougal That's right. Thirst was the biggest problem.

Douglas We drank liquid from the spines of fish!

Neil And turtles' blood.

Journalist 2 Can you tell us how you were rescued?

Dougal Well I decided to head . . .

Neil It was a Japanese fishing boat.

Douglas But Dad would've got us there anyway — we were only 300 miles from land.

Dougal You see, the wind and currents were both in our favour. There was land to the west but it was too far away and . . .

Journalist 2 What about shipping lanes?

Dougal Oh, no point in waiting to be rescued, you see, because no one knew we were missing, and we were miles from the shipping lanes. So north-east we went.

Lyn But the fishing boat only crossed our path by a series of coincidences.

Douglas We had tons of turtle meat and water at the end.

Neil They said we stank.

Lyn They'd had engine trouble, fuel problems and then a change of instructions from the owners.

Dougal Anyway *I* was glad to see them.

Journalist 3 Weren't you afraid of sharks? Did you come across any?

Neil Yeah, lots.

Douglas We caught one and ate it!

Lyn They were more of a problem because they ate our fishing bait or took the fish off the line as soon as we caught them.

Dougal Yeah, they never actually attacked us.

Journalist 1 Did you really eat raw turtle meat?

Douglas Oh yes, and their eggs.

Neil They were so nosey they swam right up to the boat!

Lyn And flying fish that landed in the boat.

Dougal And finally we made a spear to catch fish with, to foil the sharks.

Journalist 3 You spent 38 days in that boat, is that right?

Dougal Yeah, but we were kept pretty busy.

Neil Mum made us do exercises.

Douglas We had to keep a look-out all the time.

Lyn Empty the boat of water.

Dougal And we were always trying to catch fish.

Lyn And we passed the time dreaming about food.

All Mmmm!

Dougal We imagined we were going to a restaurant back home.

Douglas And we thought of all the fantastic dishes we'd have on the menu.

Neil Turtle's blood.

Lyn Neil!

Journalist 2 And what are your plans now? Everything you owned was in that sailing boat.

Dougal We're off to the best restaurant in town.

Journalist Oh, there's a very good fish . . .

Douglas & Lyn Not on your life!

Homework

Date	Task	Completed	Error and correction

Notes

Notes

Acknowledgements

Acknowledgements are made to the following writers and publishers who have allowed us to use material that falls within their copyright:

Douglas Adams and Pan Books for extracts from *The Hitchhiker's Guide to the Galaxy*; The *Athenian* magazine for an article on the Rights of Women in Greece; the estate of W H Auden and Faber and Faber for 'The Unknown Citizen' from *Collected Poems*; Keith H Basso and the *Journal of Anthropological Research* for an article 'To Give up on Words: Silence in Western Apache Culture' (Vol. 26, No. 3); Patricia Beer for the poem 'Gorilla' from *The Survivors*; the estate of Dr J Bronowski and Curtis Brown Ltd for an extract 'Leonardo and his times' from *The Western Intellectual Tradition*; C Brooks and R Warren for an extract from *Modern Rhetoric*, Shorter Third Edition, copyright © 1972 by Harcourt Brace Jovanovich, Inc. Reprinted by permission of the publisher; Canon (UK) Ltd for their Canon T50 advertisement; Citalia for their advertisement; Anita Desai and William Heinemann for an extract from *Fire on the Mountain*; Robin Dunbar and the New Scientist for an article appearing in *New Scientist*, London (12 Jan 1984); the estate of William Faulkner and Chatto and Windus: The Hogarth Press for extracts from *Soldier's Pay*; John Hill and Oxford Illustrated Press for an extract from *Dry Slope Ski-ing*; David Holbrook and the Anvil Press for the poem 'Me and the Animals' from *Selected Poems, 1980*; G Leech and Longman for an extract 'English in Advertising' from *The Longman Companion to English Literature* (ed. C. Gullie); Newsweek Inc. for an extract from *Newsweek Encyclopaedia of Family Health*; Christine Nutall and William Heinemann for an extract from *Teaching Reading Skills in a Foreign Language*; the Open University and Longman for an extract from *Personality, Growth and Learning*; the estate of Mrs Sonia Brownell Orwell and Secker and Warburg for extracts from *Animal Farm* by George Orwell; Penguin Books Ltd for an extract from the cover blurb of *Animal Farm*; Rank Xerox for their advertisement; Dougal Robertson and Grafton Books for an extract from *Survive the Savage Sea*; Roger Rosenblatt for an article 'A Glorious Ritual' (*Time* Magazine August 6, 1984), reprinted by permission of Time Inc; Gamini Salgado and J M Dent and Sons Ltd for an extract from *The Elizabethan Underworld*; N F Simpson and Faber and Faber for an extract from *One Way Pendulum*; Ric Sissoons and the New Socialist magazine for an article 'Batting on the Brink' (*New Socialist* August 1983); Spare Rib for an article on women and self-defence in the *Spare Rib Reader*; the Spanish Tourist Authority for their advertisement; Tim Severin and Europress Ltd for an article '30 Days' (Europress 1984); Tim Severin, Rolex and J Walter Thompson for an extract adapted from a Rolex advertisement; the Societé Encyclopaedique Universelle for an extract from the Longman-Pears Encyclopaedia; C O Trake and the *American Anthropologist* for an adaptation of an article 'How to ask for a drink in Subanun' (*American Anthropologist* 66:6, Part 2, 1964. Not for further reproduction); R Thomson and Penguin Books Ltd for an extract from *The Psychology of Thinking*; Andrew Wright for his anecdote from *Moments, A Collection of Short Stories* (Pilgrims 1978); D Wilkins and Oxford University Press for an extract from *Notional Syllabuses*; World Wildlife Fund (UK) for their advertisement.

The publishers would also like to thank the following for their permission to reproduce photographs:

Barbican Centre, Tim Batstone, BBC Enterprises, Camera Press, Canon UK Ltd, The J. Allan Cash Photo Library, Mary Evans Picture Library, John Egan/Jason Voyage, Format, Sally and Richard Greenhill, The Ronald Grant Archive, William Heinemann Ltd, Keystone Collection, The Kobal Collection, The National Film Institute, Network, Penguin Books Ltd, Popperfoto, Rex Features, Telefocus/British Telecom Photo Library

Location photography by:

Rob Judges

Cover illustration by:

Johnathan Field

Illustrations by:

Alex Brychta, Ray Burrows, Andy Bylo, John Cooper, Amanda Li, Maggie Ling, Francis Lloyd, Karen Ludlow, Michael Manning, Kim Raymond, RDH Artists, Michael Renouf, Axel Scheffler, Laura Simmonds, Hany Tamba, Paul Thomas, Tony Watson